Wm. J. Schaldach

WHITE RIVER, VERMONT, etching, bitten line, size 6" x 8", unpublished, 1940

The Wind on Your Cheek

OR

MORE CHIPS FROM THE LOG OF AN ARTIST SPORTSMAN

William J. Schaldach

WITH AN INTRODUCTION BY ARNOLD GINGRICH

Freshet Press
ROCKVILLE CENTRE,
NEW YORK

OTHER BOOKS BY WILLIAM SCHALDACH

FISH BY SCHALDACH   CARL RUNGIUS

CURRENTS & EDDIES   UPLAND GUNNING

COVERTS & CASTS   PATH TO ENCHANTMENT

Special acknowledgments must be made to several publishers for permission to reprint material first printed elsewhere. "To Filch A Fish" first appeared in *Fishing Waters of the World;* "The Dark of the Moon" was first published in *Hunting and Fishing* magazine; "Net Results," "Grousing Is Easy," "Old Ragged Fin," and "Jonathan Woodcock, Esq.," were originally published in *Field & Stream.*

Library of Congress Catalog Card Number: 72-81480
Manufactured in the United States of America

To my dear ones—Jo, Marni, Virginia, and Bill, Jr., with fond recollections of our many delightful wanderings in the outdoors.

Contents

SALMON LEAPING A WATERFALL, dry point, size 5⅜" x 8⅞", published in 1928, edition of 50

Introduction

THE art in angling is, I am afraid, a lot more important than angling in art. As everyone knows who has ever seen a copy of Sparrow's *Angling in British Art,* there have been a great many fine anglers who were artists but very few fine artists who were anglers. Of course, there have been thousands of books spawned by the sport over the last five centuries, and most of them have been illustrated, but out of hundreds of angling artists, only a handful have attained master status as artist anglers.

Rowlandson and Turner, yes. Both were great artists, and both frequently treated angling subjects. Landseer, Raeburn, Alma-Tadema . . . and in America, Winslow Homer and John Singer Sargent—it's hard to muster a glittering galaxy of names. Also sad but true is the fact that the better the artist the fewer the angling pictures by him.

But the paucity of fine artist anglers is as nothing compared to the scarcity of angling artists who are also angling authors. Try to find a blend of artist, angler, and author in anything like a reasonable balance; if you succeed, you have a very rare specimen indeed.

In England there is Bernard Venables, and here we had—alas, not for long—John Atherton. There remains, praise be, William J. Schaldach.

On all three counts, as artist, author, and angler, Bill Schaldach passes anybody's test. But when you add the fourth dimension, which is artistry with the gun as well as the rod, then the man begins to stretch the corners of credulity, and you start to wonder, with the farmer at his first sight of a giraffe, whether there can indeed be any such creature.

There is and has been, as I can attest, over the span of very nearly forty years, to my own knowledge and great satisfaction.

William J. Schaldach began to glorify the pages of *Esquire* with words and pictures invoking rods and guns almost before the magazine was out of its swaddling clothes, and he remained one of the chief ornaments of its sporting side through its vintage years.

He warmed the cockles of this manic angler's heart as far back as May of 1936 by pointing out that "one has only to see a skillful performer casting a fly to appreciate that the sport has in it the elements of art. And an artist thinks seriously about his tools . . . the angler has much the same feeling for his rod as that possessed by a violinist for a rare Amati or Guarnerius."

But even more endearing, to me, because it's more enduring, is this tenet of the Schaldach dogma, as laid down away back in those days before we'd ever heard of glass rods or floating lines or nylon tippets: "One of the reasons that fly-fishing appeals to so many men, I think, is that the sport is non-competitive. There are occasional individuals, I know, who can't seem to be happy unless they go forth for the day's fishing laden with bets on the first fish, the largest fish, the heaviest creel, and so on. Such men miss the point. Angling is an aesthetic pleasure."

Introduction

There speaks the kind of man who can give a sport a good name. And angling is indeed an aesthetic pleasure as practiced and preached and portrayed in such books as *Currents & Eddies* and *Coverts & Casts* and no less in this new one.

Here, in every line of the pictures as well as in every line of the prose, there is the inimitable authority and the sure hand of the veteran, who has kept his eyes and his mind open to every new experience and every sensation of ever-recurring wonder. This last is the difference between the days spent out of doors by the sensitive artist and the unthinking clod. Some men could go through the same motions, over the same grounds, and come back with nothing but some meat and a monosyllabic grunt. Others would talk your head off without conveying the least idea of what if was like to be there. Some can make you feel what it was like. Of this gifted company is Schaldach. But better yet, with him, you can see it too, not only once but again and again.

He dates from the days of the untreated split-cane rods that you had to coddle constantly to keep from acquiring a "set," of the gut tippets that you had to soak between felt pads overnight to avoid snapping your fly off on the first cast, of the silk lines that you had to take off the reel and wind around a line-dryer (or a chair-back) to avert the damp-rot that would let a little fish become a tackle-buster—he dates, indeed, from those good old days that we marvel now that we could ever have enjoyed.

But his art is ageless, and his viewpoint is as eternally fresh, with this book's many exemplifications of its recurrent motif of "You never can tell," as a tug on your line, or a sudden whir of wings behind you, or, indeed, the wind on your cheek.

—Arnold Gingrich

11

Foreword

IN THIS rapidly changing world, lovers of angling and shooting are inclined to take a pessimistic view of the future. We are faced with many obstacles that seem insurmountable—the steady increase of population, the pollution of air and waters, the destruction of forests, marshlands and wildlife cover, and the greed of commercial fisheries—for example, the alarming decline of the Atlantic salmon—to name only a few.

Happily, there are signs that the situation is not entirely irreversible. Conservation organizations, influential sportsmen's groups, and alarmed private individuals are rallying to the cause and doing all they can to preserve our natural heritage and that of our children. Except in remote areas, we may have to be content with angling for artificially reared fish and shooting stocked birds, but if we persist, the picture will not be as gloomy as it sometimes seems.

The instinct for hunting and fishing lies deep within us. It dates back to the origins of true man, many thousands of years ago, when obtaining animals, birds, and fish was a daily necessity to maintain life. This instinct has come down to us through the ages and will never be erased. Primitive traits are never entirely lost; the dog turns around three times before settling down to sleep—remember?

We shall never be able to return to the days, no more distant than the beginning of the twentieth century, when wild game and fish teemed in many parts of our land and posted land was rarely encountered; when laws were liberal and seasons long.

By the late 1940s a steady change was taking place. Each year more fishing and hunting licenses were issued, and books and magazines dealing with sport appeared like mushrooms. Alas, the supply of fish and game couldn't keep up the pace, and we have reached the point where we now stand—at an impasse until ecological science steps in and at least partially remedies matters.

But we old-timers, though our joints may creak and we are no longer able to indulge in the strenuous sports we love, have one thing to fall back on—memories of wonderful days in the open.

This is nostalgia, a precious thing on which this book is based. May it also inspire the younger generation of sportsmen who at times wonder if it is all over. Be of good cheer; it isn't if we all pitch in and do our part. There is yet time.

The chapters in this book are from pieces written in the 1930s, '40s, and early '50s. Five of these have appeared in magazines; the remaining three have not previously been published. They are largely based on the author's personal experiences or on tales told by his friends.

The events recorded are basically true, but it is well known that the sportsman (especially the angler) moves in a delightful world

Foreword

of fantasy, away from the practicalities of city life. He can be forgiven if, at times, his enthusiasm leads him to stretch cold fact just a trifle and imagine, with a chuckle, things that *might* happen; sometimes a two-pound trout grows magically with the years into a five-pounder!

You know that there is much more to your days in the open than flushing wings and rising trout, and these are some of the things that are remembered: the song of the vesper sparrow at evening; the musical gurgle of running water; the fragrance of damp poplar leaves on the ground as you follow your questing dog.

And, as a tonic to body and soul, the wind on your cheek.

W.J.S.
Tubac, Arizona
January, 1972

'COON HOLLOW, *pen and wash drawing, size 8" x 11", unpublished*

# Gentle Loafer

Gentle Loafer

ONE late October afternoon in the grouse covers of west Michigan I met my teacher, the man who was to be my guide and counselor in the mysteries of wildlife and sport in the open for several happy years. He came at a moment of deep despair, like a prophet in the desert.

I had hunted long and hard that day and, after a succession of miserable misses, had finally knocked down a big grouse. When I looked for the bird it wasn't there. Only some scuffed earth and a couple of feathers showed where it had struck. After several minutes' search in widening circles I heard footsteps. A man, followed by a dog, stepped out of a patch of cedars. He was holding a fine grouse by one leg.

"Guess this is your bird, sonny," he said. "I was workin' the other side of this ridge when I heard your shot. Then Ned, my setter here, started trailin'. Follered for a couple hundred yards before he picked it up. Jest wing-tipped. Shootin' without a dog? Well, when you knock down a partridge you better get there as fast as them young legs'll carry you. If a bird ain't killed outright, it'll run and hide every time."

That was my first lesson in a curriculum that included such fascinating and unique subjects as hunting for pearls in fresh-water mussels, gathering ginseng, and shooting muskrats in high water in the spring—in addition to the usual academic course in straight gunning and angling.

He was tall and lean, slightly stoop-shouldered, and he walked with the rolling gait of an Indian. His face was gaunt and angular, and beneath an aquiline nose he wore a walrus mustache generous enough to conceal a fledgling sparrow. His keen gray eyes peered at you with the intentness of a hawk seeking prey, and you felt that he was looking right through you and out the other side of your skull. If your first impression was one of apprehension, it was quickly dispelled by his rich, soft voice. Actually, he was a gentle soul, and all the kids and dogs in town loved him.

His name was Lester Spooner, and he lived in the small town of Comstock Park, better known as Mill Creek, north of Grand Rapids. Everybody knew him simply as "Les," the town no-good who spent all his time roaming the woods or on some lake or stream, to the mortification of his family. This wasn't strictly the truth. Les held a steady, if undistinguished, job as night watchman in the local tannery on the nearby Grand River. He had a small house and garden, a wife, and a couple of children. They never looked emaciated to me, and Les always managed to keep out of debt.

War clouds had not yet gathered on the horizon of Europe when I met Les. Away from the cities roads were poor, and there were few automobiles. Good trout streams, upland covers, and marshes

Gentle Loafer

lay nearby, but were hard to reach. The army of gunners and fishermen had not yet begun the invasion. I was sixteen, a kid in high school with, I fear, a greater desire to learn how to hit a grouse than to find that Caesar had been swindled by Brutus.

Mill Creek was reached from our house in town by street-car. It was a long ride on the Wealthy-Scribner line and cost a nickel. Or I sometimes rode my bicycle, carrying gun or rod and creel on my back. As my friendship for Les increased I spent every available day with him in some delightful adventure. Friends of mine who knew the man—the exterior side only—used to warn me that if I kept up that sort of thing I'd be just like him, a bum and a loafer. But their protestations left me cold. I felt that I was getting something they never would have; and now that I look back I know it.

With a week end off I'd go to Mill Creek after school and find Les at his house. I would bring bread, butter, and a couple of cans of vegetables, but there were always more interesting things to eat. It might be fried muskrat hams, rabbit, or grouse; fat mallard or teal; or great chunks of silver catfish, fresh from the river. A couple of times we had delicious steaks that tasted suspiciously like venison. It wasn't deer season, but I asked no questions. If Les was a poacher, I figured it was none of my business.

Les went on duty at the tannery at 7:00 p.m. I'd go with him, and we would talk until about ten o'clock; then I would throw a blanket over a pile of tanned horsehides, pull another over on top, and pass out peacefully. It wasn't a bad bed at that—if you could stand the odor. To me, the sharp pungency of oak-tanned leather was more exquisite than the most expensive Paris perfume. Mother couldn't see it that way. When I'd get home she would order me into the tub and seize my clothes with evident disgust. She used to swear that it took three days' airing in the sun to freshen them.

BARNHART'S POOL, BEAVERKILL, *dry point, size 8¾" x 11¾", published in 1929, edition of 50*

Les' job was to stoke the fires under the boilers a couple of times a night and to see that no prowlers gained access to the place. He had a broken-down old Morris chair, concealed in a corner, in which he spent a good many hours surreptitiously dozing. But, cat-like, he would awaken at the slightest sound, and nothing escaped his vigilance. When I was to be there for an adventure on the following day, he always managed enough sleep to be bright and eager in the morning.

In the fall it would be a hunt for partridge and woodcock in the covers up along Strawberry Creek; or if it happened to be his "day off," we'd take an early-morning train for Edgerton or Cedar Springs on the Grand Rapids & Indiana (Go Ragged and Independent, Les called it) or the Père Marquette. Birds were everywhere in those days, and seldom did we return without a good bag. Les killed most of them, of course, but under his tutelage I gradually learned how to hit more and miss less.

Or it might be a foray in one of the three big marshy wonderlands near Mill Creek—Gunn, Baily, and Comstock. If there had been a blow out of the north the night before and the morning came off bright and frosty, the wet meadowlands and boggy spots along numerous little creeks were invariably popping with jacksnipe. Les was a marvelous shot, both with rifle and smoothbore, and he was particularly deadly on the twisting, dodging little jack. His formula for hitting them was simple—if you could follow it. "Always hunt with the wind on your back," he advised, "and the snipe will jump into it to rise. Then he'll turn and usually take a long quarterin' swing before he tacks. That's the time to pull. If you don't get 'im then, wait till he straightens out."

One memorable day after a cold, windy night, we sloshed through the frosty grass and bog of Comstock Marsh to find snipe

Gentle Loafer

everywhere. They flew in wisps of half a dozen and jumped from every likely-looking spot. I was beginning to get the hang of it and was shooting pretty well. Les, of course, was simply decimating the ranks. At a "cathole," a little pond surrounded by cattails, I had the luck to jump a big greenhead mallard and kill him. Les shortly picked up two greenwing teal. We had shot for about three hours when it dawned on us that our game pockets were getting heavy and our shells were about exhausted.

"Willie," Les said—he always called me Willie—"do you know how many birds you got?" I told him that I hadn't kept count. "Well, neither have I," he replied, "but we better quit. I wouldn't want Jack Johnson [the local game warden] to ast me any embarrassin' questions. Him and me is on pretty good terms, and I figger it best to keep it that way."

We went home, and Les dumped the combined bag into a big galvanized bucket. The top was rounded off with snipe like an exotic frosting. Since a jack weighs a bare four ounces, it looked like a game hog's job, and it would have been, except that the snipe were bedded down by the mallard and the two teal.

Les was an instinctive gunner; he had never had any training at traps or on the rifle range. But some of the shots he pulled off bordered on the miraculous. One day late in September we were fishing for channel cats in his skiff on the Grand River. A flock of six Canada geese circled and dropped into a little cove fully 200 yards off. Les quietly reached for his .22 rifle, an old-fashioned, heavy, single-shot weapon with falling-block action. He slipped in a long-rifle cartridge—in those days they were loaded with semismokeless, or "Lesmok" powder—and snaked down into the bottom of the skiff to get a rest. After studying for a moment, he rested the rifle on the gunwale of the skiff, sighted, and pulled. At the spat of the explosion

27

JUMPING JACK-SNIPE, dry point, size 6" x 7¼", published in 1928, edition of 50

five geese jumped, but one remained. A big honker had been hit squarely in the head!

I was dumfounded and told Les so. He took it as a matter of course; he had expected to hit. "Shucks, it ain't nothin', Willie," he said simply. "You jest sight on the bird, h'ist 'er up a leetle to 'low for elevation, and tech 'er off." There you have the formula for hitting a goose at 200 yards—in case you're interested.

Except for about three months of deep winter, I joined Les at every opportunity for whatever was in season. He was much devoted to trout fishing, and he tied his own flies and devised some startling tackle. Although he owned a "boughten" fly rod of split bamboo, he rarely used it, preferring a creation of his own. It consisted of three joints of Calcutta cane, each four feet long, joined together with brass ferrules. He fashioned a reel seat of brass, and whipped on ring-and-keeper guides, finally painting it with dark forest-green bicycle enamel. This had chipped off in mottled patches, leaving the yellow bamboo showing in irregular spots. Les affectionately called this weapon the Spotted Adder. With it he could cast a fly an amazing distance, skitter a spoon, or simply bait-fish.

One evening he had been sitting patiently for an hour, immobile as a bronze General Grant, trying to lure a big bass with a live minnow. "You know what happened?" he asked. I didn't.

"Danged kingfisher plopped down on my pole, tettered a second, dived in the water, and came up with a minnie—my minnie."

"What did you do?" I asked.

"Hmmm. Packed off for home. Figgered it was about time!"

Les eked out his slender wages by living off the woods and waters. But he regarded everything he did as sport; that's why he chose the occupation of night watchman—so he'd have plenty of daylight hours in which to roam. Not only was there game and fish on the table at all times to save butcher's bills, but there were also many other things. His wife would have a new dress or there would be toys for the kids. "Found a nice bunch of gingshang," he'd say with a grin, "better'n three pounds, and it fetched eight dollars a pound." He showed me how to look for the rare plant, so valued by the Chinese; to spot the red berries before frost comes, and the tribranched stem, each stalk with five leaves.

Or it might be pearls. There was a regular industry on the Grand River in dredging up fresh-water mussels, the shells of which furnished the raw material for a pearl-button factory. Spooner had his own little rig, and we'd trawl certain beds he knew, open the mollusks, and eagerly look for pearls. Mostly we'd find slugs or seed pearls, but on one happy day Les opened a "clam" and found a perfect gem, a fine pearl the size of a pea. He later sold it to a jeweler for eighty dollars and bought himself an N. R. Davis double hammerless 12-gauge shotgun.

Les was an eager and accomplished trapper, and I'd often accompany him when he'd run his line. He caught raccoon, fox, mink, "mushrat," weasel, and skunk. He showed me how to set for all these animals, and for a time I ran a small line of my own in the country south of town. But trapping never appealed to me much, especially as I had to get up at 4:00 a.m., pedal my bike five miles each way, and get cleaned up for an 8:30 class at school. I concentrated on muskrat and did pretty well. A prime 'rat brought 60 cents, and with shotgun shells—the best, loaded with Du Pont or Schultz smokeless—selling at 50 cents a box (!) a few pelts a week gave me a lot of shooting.

I shied clear of skunks, having a social standing of sorts to maintain; and weasels, which are "ermine" in the winter, are practically as bad—if you are on the skinning instead of the wearing end. A king or a fine lady wouldn't know about that. An adventure I had

Gentle Loafer

Net Results

Net Results

FROM the time he was six years old, Jones had been an inveterate angler, and almost up to the day of his passing, at the ripe old age of eighty-two, he pursued the trout, bass, and salmon with the fervor of youth. His domestic and business life had been exemplary, but uncharitable individuals accused him of shocking deviations from the straight line of truth in relating his fishing adventures. Some people are that way.

Although Jones was sincere enough himself, it was not without some trepidation that he approached the headquarters of Saint Peter. Things went along smoothly enough until they got on the subject of angling.

"Fishing?" the good saint inquired, brightening noticeably. "Tell me about it. I used to be a fisherman myself."

37

Jones took courage. "Well, I spent a lot of time at it and did pretty well, on the whole. But people never would believe the stories I told. They said that I lied like—excuse me, like everything. I suppose the things I told them did sound fantastic, but—"

"For example?"

"Oh, there was that eight-pound brown trout I caught in the Battenkill on a four-X leader and three-ounce rod. I had lost my net, and it was getting dark. I was in a tough spot and—"

"But the trout really did weigh eight pounds, didn't it?"

"Well-l-l—"

"Of course, of course. And it was a three-ounce rod?"

"Mm, the rod weighed—"

"How exciting! Just think of that! It's a pity more people don't take up fishing; I'm sure there would be much less trouble on the old earth. Pass right on, friend."

Fishing is not an exact science, thank heavens, and only dreadfully practical people demand mathematical accuracy—in inches and pounds. Besides, just what is accuracy? It is not easy to be absolutely sure. There is the case of that big squaretail I once saw hooked and played on a certain stream in Maine.

The angler was a noted fly fisherman who could do things with a four-ounce rod that would make the average man turn green with envy. He was working a little backwater across the river, using a small bucktail. The distance was fully ninety feet, and the line would slip out in a manner very pretty to see. His rod tightened into an arc as he struck, and the fight was on.

It looked like a good fish, and out of curiosity I glanced at my watch. After many dogged runs and much stubborn boring, the trout gave in and was led close to the sandy shore. There he lay in the water, tired out and gently fanning the current with his white-edged

Net Results

carmine fins. Two experienced guides were handy, ready to net him.

"Want to keep him, Bob?" one of them asked.

"No, let him go. What'll he weigh?"

"Three pounds," one of the guides said.

The other nodded in assent.

I looked at my watch. Exactly seven minutes had passed since the trout took.

The following winter I ran into this fisherman in New York at the Sportsman's Show. "Do you remember that big squaretail you hooked in the Dunkelbunk Stream last fall?" I asked.

"Do I remember him? Judas Priest, what a fish? What a fight! Six pounds flat, and forty-five minutes to lick him. Wasn't he an old socker!"

Who am I to say that the trout didn't weigh six pounds? Nobody weighed him. And it is entirely possible that I read the time wrong. Things like that have happened. You see what I mean?

Anglers are great indulgers in wishful thinking, and one has only to wrap his hand around the grip of a rod and hear the click of a reel to understand why. Fishing is a romantic sport, and anything that contributes to the happiness of the angler should not be denied him. There are bigger fish in the stream than have ever been caught, and your true disciple remains ever hopeful. If he has to wait too long, can he be blamed for helping matters along a little—in one way or another? Remember, he has a reputation to maintain. Here is a perfect example:

During a dozen years of fishing on the Beaverkill the biggest trout I ever ran across weighed in the neighborhood of 11 pounds. He was a surprisingly shapely brown, about a yard long. This was no mythical fish—that kind often weigh twice as much—but could be seen in all his plaster-of-Paris and oak-paneled glory, hanging on the wall of the local hotel, in a town where fisherman gathered.

While the mounting job wasn't bad, the color was atrocious —a dead oyster white on the belly and up the side, then greenish mud blending into a rich ox-blood shoe polish. Whoever painted the thing had heard that trout have spots, so he used his imagination liberally and, with loving care, sprinkled it from head to tail with myriads of enlarged commas, exclamation points, asterisks, and periods—all of them black. For good measure he threw in a few dimes and nickels of a hue employed in decorating fire engines.

From the mouth of this wondrous creature there protruded a truly impressive Parmachene Belle, size 2/0, tied to a piece of leader strong enough to tow a log raft in a stiff breeze. Fishermen came from far and wide to gaze upon this incredible object. The proprietor politely answered all questions and stoutly maintained that the great trout had been caught by so-and-so (long deceased) "on that very rig." The locality was always "down river," which, of course, covers a lot of territory.

The more polite brothers simply wrinkled their brows and murmured, "Hmmm!" Some outspoken individuals expressed open skepticism, and this never failed to grieve the mild-mannered little proprietor.

One hot June day I was sitting on the long veranda, talking with a couple of fishermen and awaiting the late afternoon and the fly hatch. The proprietor beckoned me over furtively, and we went into the privacy of his office. He had something on his mind.

"That trout on the wall," he began. "It's a terrible paint job. Now I've seen you sketching around here, and I'm wondering if maybe you could do him over and make him look like something."

"I could," I replied, "but you will have to do something in return. Tell me just where that critter came from."

Net Results

"Why, you've heard the story a dozen times. You believe it, don't you?" He was beginning to get that hurt tone in his voice, which, from long practice, sounded very professional.

"Of course, I know the story. The trout was caught down river on a Parmachene Belle fly by so-and-so, who is now deceased. I believe every word of it, especially the part about the fly. In fact, the two-o Parmachene is almost my favorite. Darn good pattern. I catch all my big trout on it. And besides, I believe every fishing story I hear. Make a practice of it. Now, just between the two of us, where did that shark hail from, and how did you come by him?"

Being desperately eager to have the fish painted, he gave up without an argument. The huge trout was found dead in an eddy near Cook's Falls in a perfectly fresh condition. Whether his demise was brought about by pollution from an acid factory or just plain old age no one knew. He was iced and rushed to the city for mounting, being returned a couple of months later with the dolorous color effect previously noted. There was plenty of time to weave a story which, though vague, had undoubted charm. After all, finding a dead trout and having him mounted is a pretty dull thing. Why not make the boys feel good if it lies in one's power? Now I'm sure that you see what I mean.

Every follower of the craft is, in some measure, a dreamer and a romanticist. If this were not so, he would go in for golf or some sport where the factors are pretty well known. But on stream or lake the unknown lies just ahead. It may be a great bald eagle, soaring over a towering cliff; a mother bear with a couple of cubs; a moose with antlers in the velvet, feeding on lily pads; or one of a host of things which have nothing to do with fishing. It may even be a spot of danger that furnishes the added tang of adventure to any fishing trip, and is an ever-present possibility. Consider a well-remembered

41

day I had on the upper reaches of the Willowemoc years ago.

It was late in June, and the best fishing on the big water had passed. Pop Robbins, the Dean of the Beaverkill, suggested that we take a mutual friend, drive to Conkling's covered bridge, and fish the river where it is small. The water remains cool in that section, and trout will take a dry fly long after they have quit down below. It was tricky fishing because of the clear water, but with care an angler would usually be well repaid.

I drove my car to the bridge, where I was dropped off, and they went on to Willowemoc Village to fish above the town. It was about a mile and a half by stream, a leisurely day's fishing through a lonely and beautiful wooded stretch of country. I was to meet them at around five o'clock.

Though it was fairly hot, a gentle breeze drove occasional fleecy clouds across an azure-blue sky. I had never fished the stretch before, and the prospect was intriguing. As I strung up, a good rise disturbed the water near the stone abutment of the old covered bridge. Moss-green rings widened, their upturned facets reflecting the deep blue of the sky.

Now, there is something about a bridge—especially a covered bridge—which is simply irresistible to a fly fisherman. Everybody knows that the biggest trout in the stream always lives under a bridge, and you have the feeling that you're going to be lucky enough to catch him. The fact that you never do doesn't mean a thing.

False-casting a couple of times, I dropped the little Pink Lady bivisible over the rise I had seen. A golden flash warmed the cool shadows, and the fly disappeared in a spatter of drops. It was a 10-inch brown, and I was off to a good start.

Fishing along the little river was pleasant, and several more trout, both browns and brooks, found their way into the creel. Then

Net Results

I remembered Pop's injunction to watch out for a sinkhole that could get me into trouble. It was on the right-hand side of the stream, he said, about a half mile above the bridge. It was plainly marked with a warning sign and could be avoided easily if I kept vigilant.

A sinkhole in a river is caused by a spring that boils out of the stream bed, making a rotten bottom. You can seldom spot one by looks, as the action of both the stream and the spring keeps the gravel, sand, or marl in motion and conceals the trouble. Since this sinkhole was on the right side of the stream, I figured I would be perfectly safe if I kept along the left side. Besides, there would be that sign.

Continuing to wade and cast, I reached a spot where an inviting run gurgled along a moss-draped ledge. I placed a floater at the lower end, retrieved, stripped a couple more yards of line from the reel and cast higher up. Without looking, I took another step. Then it happened!

Instantly my left leg plunged almost to the boot top in bottomless silt and gravel. I lost my balance, and my right leg collapsed under me, but as it was on firm bottom I threw my weight in that direction and fell flat in the stream bed. The water, fortunately, was only a few inches deep, and after some struggle I managed to worm my foot and leg out of the left boot, leaving it in the sinkhole. There was enough rubber protruding to recover the boot—after I had regained my wits and breath. All the while I had been hanging for dear life onto a piece of ancient barbed wire which stretched across the stream from one bank to another.

Making my way along this wire, I came upon a piece of board, at the outer edge of the marl bed, stapled to the fencing. It was partly submerged, and I fished it out and read: "Danger! Sink Hole." There was the sign, all right, but not in a position to do any good. It had been many years since Pop had fished that stretch, and in the

43

meantime the little river had shifted its course enough to leave the danger spot on the left side of the stream.

I fixed the sign up as well as I could without tools. Then, out of curiosity, I cut a long alder and poked it into the sinkhole. It went down for many feet with very little resistance, giving me an exceedingly creepy feeling. If you are ever up that way, remember the sinkhole. It is—or was—about a half mile above Conkling's covered bridge. It's on the left-hand side of the stream; or it might be on the right-hand side, or possibly in the middle. And there is a good chance that there won't be any sign.

The veranda of that country hotel in the Catskill Mountains, back in those days, was the brew pot of many an adventure. There, weird and fantastic fly patterns were evolved, and the theory and mechanics of fly-fishing practice were ironed out daily to a starched-shirt smoothness. Some of the ideas advanced were so delightfully nutty that they amused everyone but their propounders. Armchair fishing always intensified in direct ratio to a falling-off of sport on the river.

When the boys came back with empty creels after a hard day's wading, they laid it to their technique and figured that maybe a little concentrated thinking with the aid of a slide rule would turn the trick. Most of it was wasted effort, but one bright boy came through nobly, and from him I learned something that I had never known before.

He was a long, lanky fellow who hailed from New Jersey. He had heard of the Beaverkill's fame and wanted to try the river. But it was late in the season, with hot weather and no fly hatches. A dozen anglers hung on, hoping for a rain which would raise the river and put the fish back on the feed. Meanwhile they fished diligently and talked mightily, in an effort to find some way of changing their luck.

Net Results

The stranger sat silently through the conversation. He was a good listener, but didn't advance any theories. At the end of his first day on the stream he climbed up on the porch, stripped off his waders, and dumped such a creelful of trout out onto the floor as to shock us all mute and popeyed. He was polite but reticent, giving evasive answers to questions.

The next day the same thing happened, to the consternation and wonderment of everyone. That evening I talked with him for some time. We discussed rods, lines, flies, the stream—everything but what I wanted most to know, which was, of course, how under the sun he had taken those fish when it just couldn't be done. Seeing that I wasn't going to prod him, he volunteered to take me along next day and let me in on the secret.

We met early the following morning at an appointed rendezvous and struck through the woods to a point on the river considerably above the more popular stretches. The dry spell hung on, and a hot sun blazed down on a stream that shrank by the hour. I had fished this piece of water many times before, using fine leaders and tiny flies and the utmost casting skill I could command, but with practically no results. It was with considerable interest, therefore, that I watched my lanky acquaintance string up his tackle.

He attached a tapered leader with 3X point to his line, opened his fly box, and produced a huge fan-wing Royal Coachman, tied on a No. 8 hook, with wings fully as big as those on a cabbage butterfly. I thought he was nuts, and I continued to think so as he approached a fast rip which boiled a foot high over a gravel bed. He walked right up to it boldly and stepped into the water at the lower end.

"Watch this," he said as the line shot out and the big fan-wing dropped not fifteen feet away.

Wham! The fly was engulfed practically as it lit, and a 12-inch brownie was led to the net after a stiff scrap.

Net Results

"Now you try it at the upper end of the rip," he suggested.

Without much faith I dropped my fan-wing, using a short cast. Instantly the water boiled, and I was fast to a tough 10-incher. Well, this was it! Mine not to reason why. I had only seen what I had seen, but I wondered if it would last. It did.

We spent a long day on the river, covering a big strip of water. We fished only the fastest, heaviest rips, using always a short cast. If a fish didn't take at once, he wouldn't take; we proved that pretty thoroughly. At day's end our creels were heavy, and the boys on the porch had a very bad dose of green-eyed-monster trouble.

The explanation is simple, and the stranger had it figured out long before on tough metropolitan-district streams. When the water gets low in hot weather, any fish inclined to feed will seek highly aerated water—which means rips. These are also natural food lanes. A trout lying out in fast water has to strike quickly or not at all; consequently he has no time to be choosy. He either smacks a drifting insect or he lets it pass. If he has too much time in which to think it over, he will refuse a fly; hence the value of a short cast. And the big fan-wing travels high and buoyantly in the water. I have tried the system again and again in widely separated places, and it has never let me down. So there it is—for free—if you haven't already discovered it for yourself.

Some philosophical soul once said, "It is not all of fishing to fish." Not having elaborated further, he might have been referring to the incredible adventures which we anglers have, or the screwy ideas we think up, or even the fabulous, delightful yarns which we have a reputation for concocting.

Whatever the meaning, he certainly had something!

47

A CHANCE FOR A DOUBLE, dry point, size 8" x 11", published in 1940, edition of 50

Woodland Drummer

A Glimpse at the Private Life of the Ruffed Grouse

Woodland Drummer

THE musical gurgle of running water sluicing past a gravel bar keynoted the forest symphony that calm spring morning. The theme, supported by the notes of many small birds, suddenly came alive with drama. Close by, a drummer joined in and with gradually accelerating tempo beat out background tones in a resonant timbre.

Bup—bup—bup—bup—bup—br-r-r-r-r-r-r-r.

Starting slowly, the sound increased into a long roll and stopped suddenly. It boomed through the trees with a strangely muffled sound.

Cedar Creek in Michigan was one of my favorite trout streams years ago, and through long acquaintance I had come to know every pool, run, and riffle in it. I also knew of this traditional old drumming log, which lay a short distance from the stream. Quietly laying down my fly rod and creel, I stalked cautiously toward the log. Spring was in the air. Anemones, violets, and adder's tongues carpeted the earth, and fragrant arbutus blossoms made pink accents in beds of leathery green leaves. And spring was in the blood of wild creatures. It was the season of love—and equally of war. If I were lucky, I might witness a rare woodland drama.

Shortly the old cock grouse sounded off again, and I made a rapid but silent and careful approach. When drumming the bird would lose his caution, and that was the time to move. He drummed at intervals as long as five minutes apart, and the stalk was a slow business.

The log was a moss-covered old patriarch that had fallen before the savagery of some long-forgotten storm. It lay in a sunny semiopen glade, surrounded by heavy undergrowth. I scarcely dared breathe as I watched the old cock strut with fan fully expanded. Keen eyes scanned the area for possible enemies, then the bird seemed to lose himself in a trance. With body rigid and partly contracted tail braced against the log he drew himself up to full height and started the slow rhythmic wing beat: *Bup—bup—bup—*

He went through the performance twice, then from among the shadowy branches of a thick hemlock the wraithlike figure of a large bird glided and landed with a plop! on the earth in front of the log. He came on silent wing, with no hint of the thundering roar a startled bird makes when flushed.

Instantly the drummer hopped off the log and made for his rival. They squared off like boxers and went at each other in a miniature whirlwind of fury. With beating wings and flying feet they flailed and hacked, scratched and pecked, giving no quarter. Feathers flew amid a cloud of dust and dead leaves. There were no Marquis of Queensbury rules; it was bare knuckles and no rounds.

Woodland Drummer

Two minutes must have passed before I noticed a movement in the brush a few feet beyond the battling birds. Then she emerged, the woman in the case. She was a demure mottled brown hen, and she paid not the slightest attention to the lovesick swains who were engaged in violent combat for her favor. She pecked idly at a wintergreen berry, stretched, and nestled down in a sunny spot for forty winks.

The sheer fury of the fight dictated its length. It ended as suddenly as it had started when the drummer, the bird that had sent out the challenge, got his rival on its back and began raking out long furrows of belly feathers. The whipped challenger slipped out from under and slunk off ingloriously. One wing was twisted a little, bloody spots showed on feathers, and he was badly tousled. The winner lacked one primary feather on a wing and needed his hair combed, but otherwise looked fit. He immediately went into a shamelessly vain strut before his queen. She idly pecked at another wintergreen berry and (I think) yawned.

A ringside seat at a grouse fight is a rare privilege and one seldom obtained; but observing a drumming grouse is not nearly so difficult—provided the prospective observer knows the location of a drumming log and possesses a reasonable degree of woodcraft and patience. Though normally one of the shyest of wild creatures, when unmolested the ruffed grouse will often live practically in one's backyard—if cover conditions are right.

Our friends, the Hamilton Merrill's, have a house on a knoll in Woodstock, Vermont. The ground falls away steeply to the north and is well wooded. A drumming log is located not more than 50 feet from the porch, down the hill, and a grouse has been coming to send out his challenge there for several years. A motion picture in color has been taken of his antics.

Woodland Drummer

The ruffed grouse, undoubtedly one of America's finest game birds, seems to be popularly regarded as falling exclusively within the province of the sportsman. This is a mistaken notion. Here is a bird not easy to know, but once its acquaintance is made the observer will reap much satisfaction. The best technique is the slow road of patience. Find a woodlot or piece of cover with feed—blackberries, wintergreen, beechnuts, weed seeds—known to be inhabited by the birds, then move with the stealth of a cat. One silent step at a time does it. Scan every old stump, laurel clump, and brushy site. The grouse is protectively colored and most difficult to spot. What actually looks like a stump may turn out to be a grouse—and vice versa! Sit down on a log near an old wood road or on a sandy spot and loaf in the sun without shame. In mid-afternoon you may be surprised to see a grouse or two walk stealthily out of the heavy cover and take a dust bath.

Fast noisy walking will flush birds well ahead, and you will see only a brown streak, accompanied by the roar of flushing wings. Slow motion does the trick. Once while fishing a trout stream I moved step by step along a cow path through some thin tag alders. The ground was soft, and I made practically no noise. Around a bend I came upon two grouse standing rigidly erect. I had approached to within two yards of them! They craned their necks and gawked at me for a full minute, then scuttled into the brush without flushing. They probably thought I was just another cow. And this was in a country that was heavily hunted in the fall.

There are many names for the ruffed grouse, and these vary according to locality. Scientifically he is known as *Bonasa umbellus*, but the New England Yankee will have no part of that; to him the bird is a "pa'tridge." Generally throughout the North he is known as "partridge," sometimes "pat," and in the mountains of Georgia and

Woodland Drummer

the Carolinas grouse are called "pheasant," which of course is a long way off the track.

The ruffed grouse has a wide distribution, ranging from the southern Appalachians to northern Canada and west to the Pacific in middle and northern states having suitable cover. It is a bird of the woodlands, but prefers cutover and second-growth land to deep forests. There are several subspecies in various parts of the country, but owing to a wide variation in color these are not easily defined.

Predominant color phases are red (rufous or foxy) and gray, similar to the phases of the screech owl. But unlike the screech owl, the grouse often shows many mixtures of color between the two dominant tones. I have seen birds with a broad tail band and ruffs—the specialized neck feathers—of pure chocolate.

The grouse is a big bird. A full grown one will average a pound and a half, and specimens weighing over two pounds have been reported. The tail, or "fan," which is the bird's glory, may spread as much as 15 inches. Sexes may be said to have identical fans, though there has been much argument about this. Old-time gunners

59

say that a clear, unbroken black tail band indicates a cock bird, but if the band is interrupted in pattern on the central feathers, the bird is a hen. Interesting if true.

The nesting season of the ruffed grouse varies somewhat according to locality, but in general it is in May. The birds are poor architects, making a crude nest of twigs on the ground. Usually it is fairly well concealed, but I recall one nest on the bank of a brook in a quite open situation. The eggs vary in number from about eight to more than a dozen.

The young chicks are fuzzy little fellows, tan in color with dark-brown and black splotches. They mind the old hen implicitly, and when danger threatens, her warning cluck freezes them into instant immobility. They are so protectively colored that they practically melt into the earth, and it is almost impossible to see them. The hen then pulls the "wounded bird" trick. She will come almost up to you, limping and dragging a wing, then slowly retreat in an attempt to lure you away from the chicks. Don't feel too sorry for her. If you follow she won't *quite* let you catch her. She will lead you a chase through thick brush and then finally sail away on strong pinions. By that time you will be a long way from where you left the chicks, and when you return they won't be there.

The grouse has many natural enemies, and the nesting season is a particularly hazardous period. Being ground nesters, the birds are open to attack from all sorts of prowling and crawling creatures. Large snakes are inordinately fond of the eggs, as are red squirrels, skunks, crows, and jays. A wet nesting season plays havoc with young birds, as this usually brings on a large crop of ticks which attach themselves to the chicks and eventually kill many of them.

By early July the young are about the size of bobwhite quail

Woodland Drummer

and can fly well enough to escape most danger. If the nesting season has been successful, a brood may number up to a dozen birds or even more. From my own field experience, covering a period of many years in several northern states and in Canada, I would say that the average brood is about eight birds.

Alternating cycles of plenty and scarcity affecting grouse have been known and recorded from as far back as Colonial times. There is no such thing as a steady supply of grouse, even though weather and nesting conditions are ideal. A cycle may run a course of from four to seven years, a gradual build-up taking place annually until every woodlot and covert is literally popping birds. Then, with unexplained suddenness, birds die off. They are frequently found dead without a mark of violence. The following year the coverts will be practically empty.

In a heavy year in good grouse country one may often flush as many as 40 or 50 birds during the course of a day's hike. This was true in 1936 and 1937 in Vermont, and again about seven years later. When the low point strikes, one may be lucky to fly three or four birds in a day. Fortunately, periods of scarcity do not coincide in all sections of the country; there may be a heavy build-up in Nova Scotia and practically no birds in Connecticut. The comeback is slow but usually noticeable from year to year.

Scientists at Cornell and other universities and the conservation commissions of several states have spent much time and effort in an attempt to solve the mystery. They have learned that the trouble is due to a combination of diseases peculiar to gallinaceous birds, and particularly to ruffed grouse, which becomes epidemic at intervals. Perhaps a method of combating them may eventually be discovered.

A tendency of the ruffed grouse seldom if ever noted in other species is an unexplainable impulse on the part of a few individuals to go "crazy," or to depart from a regular behavior pattern. This phenomenon is well known in grouse country, and each year cases are reported from various parts of the land. I have personally noted quite a number.

In a small town in Maine a grouse dove through the window of a country store, smashing a neat hole in the glass. It crawled under a counter and when released half an hour later flew off as though nothing had happened. The same thing occurred in a house in White River Junction, Vermont, right in the center of the residential district. The nearest cover was at least a half mile away. Another grouse chose a hardware store in Roscoe, New York, slamming full-tilt through a window on the main street during business hours. Strangely enough, none of these birds was so badly injured that it couldn't fly off!

One pleasant Sunday afternoon my wife and I were driving along a back-country road in Vermont. To the right a farm house was edged by an orchard. Directly opposite across the road was situated a barn with a large open door above giving entry to a hayloft. As we approached, a grouse boiled out of the orchard—for no apparent reason, as we could see no one around—crossed the road a few yards ahead of the car, and dove into the hayloft. Why, we'll never know; there was ample cover a short distance back of the barn.

Such antics might be explained by the fact that song-birds do the same thing—slam into windows regularly, thinking they can go straight through the house. They just don't know the window is there. For me that doesn't quite hold water, because the grouse is a wild woods bird, and he has no business fooling around residences

Woodland Drummer

in the center of town. However, let it go, and see what you can make of this one.

Grouseland is full of stories—all of them true—of birds that get palsy-walsy with people. Seems they are real sociable, walk up fearlessly, hop onto an outstretched arm, peck inquisitively and carry on a clucky conversation. For years I had heard of instances of this zany performance, and had even seen photographs purporting to prove it, from widely scattered sections of the country. But in spite of the evidence, it was hard to believe—until it happened to me.

Back in 1927 there was quite a stir in outdoor circles around New York about Jinny, the tame grouse of Westchester County. A number of notes and articles appeared in newspapers and magazines. I wrote one of them for a national periodical. I was pretty well qualified because Jinny was a personal friend of mine.

One day late in the fall Tom Brady of White Plains told Harold McCracken and me about this incredible bird. We drove out with Tom to the woodlot where she (he?) lived. Tom clucked with his tongue and called, "Here, Jinny, Jinny." It sounded silly, but in a couple of minutes a beautiful big grouse came coasting in, landed at our feet, and hopped up on Tom's outstretched hand. The bird walked up his arm, climbed on his shoulder, then hopped across to Harold and to me in turn. We stayed and fooled with the grouse for half an hour or more. It had no objection to being petted like a dog and would follow us when we walked around.

This was a wild bird living in a small woodlot half a mile from a house. No one had ever "tamed" it. The first intimation any-one had about the bird's abberation came to the owner of the wood-lot. He was walking there one day when a wild grouse landed ker-plunk! on his shoulder. Try to tie that one!

Jinny had all the protective instincts of a normal wild bird. It survived for several years, evading natural enemies and living through winters. It amused many people and was always home to visitors. But Jinny didn't understand traffic. One day she forgot to look up and down, and a car backed over her. (I went back to the feminine pronoun to agree with the gender of the name; but I still don't know whether Jinny was a she or a he.)

The explanation? I wouldn't know. I wonder if anyone really does.

The ruffed grouse is the Houdini of the woods, and he has as many escape tactics as were possessed by that famous magician. When in a tight corner he may fly at your head and practically knock off your hat—if he thinks that the best way out. He will put a tree trunk between you and him in a flash of whirring wings. Or he may elect to freeze and let you pass, then roar out behind you in a dazzling maneuver that makes you look slightly silly. He was in that pine tree all the time, glued up against the trunk. You missed him because you didn't look closely enough.

No doubt about it, this bird comes as close to possessing thinking brains as any wild fowl I know. That is why I am sure that, in spite of man and natural enemies, so long as there is cover left the grouse will be around a long time.

Woodland Drummer

Wm J. Schaldach

Grousing Is Easy

Grousing Is Easy

THE pursuit of the ruffed grouse is a sport that annually disrupts tempers and transforms many otherwise sweet-tempered individuals into wretched personalities. Gunners complain about the difficulties of the game. They make too hard a case of it. What they lack is plain horse sense. Here, in graphic form, are solutions to most of the harassing problems that confront the man who undertakes to follow the king of upland game birds. If he will study them faithfully and heed the instructions given, his troubles will disappear like money at a tax collector's window.

69

Grousing Is Easy

A common complaint of many gunners is that it is next to impossible to spot a bird on the ground, especially in thick brush.

Nonsense! A grouse stands about a foot high when stretched to full length, and his body is large and plump. If a man were looking for a ruby-crowned kinglet, it might be different, but what is so hard about seeing a bird the size of a spring fryer? You should be able to locate a bird any time by simply walking through the cover and keeping your eyes open. There's nothing to stop you but wild grapevines, hardhack, goldenrod stalks, dead ferns, old stubs, branches, dry leaves, and other forest items.

The next time you see a stump that looks like a grouse, but which turns out to be a grouse that looked like a stump, remind yourself that stumps don't fly. You're somewhat off in identification. Study a bird guide. By looking at the accompanying illustration from a distance of about eight feet, you will readily see how easy the problem is. You simply need more training.

Grousing Is Easy

With a little work a trained timber cruiser could estimate to a nicety the amount of firewood, in the form of limbs, shot off trees each season by poorly directed shots. It would be impressive.

Lopping off tree branches with chilled shot is a bad habit possessed by many gunners. It is not only futile but expensive—with shells selling currently at about eighteen cents apiece. Furthermore, it is wasteful, because a man has neither the time for nor the means of transporting the wood he whacks off when he is hunting. If he is woodcutting, that's one thing; but gunning is another. He should make up his mind. The saw and axe are appropriate implements for providing fuel for the home fires.

For a quick and simple solution to the problem of how to break this bad habit, we call on the science of ballistics. It offers indisputable proof that the penetration of birdshot is much, much less than the diameter of a tough old birch or pine. Furthermore, a charge of pellets whistling through the tail feathers of a grouse will do no more than urge him to press down the gas pedal a little more.

With these facts in mind you can happily dismiss the problem forever. Just remember not to shoot at birds flying behind trees. If they persist in doing it, find covers where they don't. Should this prove difficult, consult the neighborhood barber, tavern keeper, or AAA office. They're usually helpful on problems of this sort.

Nothing has been mentioned about the dog in connection with grouse hunting, because these aids to better sport are being presented for the benefit of those who are earnestly eager to learn. Dogs can't read. They don't have to; most of them are smart enough without it.

Of course, there are dogs and dogs. Let's hope you have the right kind. A well-broken dog works with the precision of machinery. He ranges at just the proper distance ahead, catches every scent no matter how dry the air, never chases rabbits, and won't point until he knows you are in a good position for a shot. He never makes a mistake. You don't have to cooperate with him; in fact, don't even give him a thought. It's his job to find birds and hold them. So cough, sneeze, holler, or sing. If you happen to be in a jovial mood, something like "Oh, What a Beautiful Morning" is appropriate.

If the dog gets nervous and busts the bird, he is a no-good, worthless brute. Get rid of him fast and buy another one. Good grouse dogs are a dime a dozen, and they run anywhere from 500 bucks on up.

Grousing Is Easy

Grousing Is Easy

The gent wearing a pained expression has made an all-too-common mistake. He was foolish enough to let a grouse get up behind him. Tsk, tsk! Bad technique.

Birds like that are hard to collect, especially when there's a flock of thick-trunked trees in the way; and when isn't there? Maybe this gunner is just inexperienced or he hasn't read enough articles on the subject. He may be weak on theory and need help. Always willing to oblige, we offer advice that we trust will be useful.

Again we appeal to the intellect in a situation that, at first glance, appears difficult but really is elementary. The gunner enters a given cover grown up to sumac, young hardwood, a few small hemlocks, and various assorted stuff. The birds—if any—are out in front somewhere. There is the cover; here is the man. Two factors. Now, it is conceivable that if the gunner walked a straight line a grouse just might skulk under a bush and wait for the fellow to pass, then roar out behind. In accordance with the most modern technique, however, this can never happen. And what a boon that is!

The solution is absurdly simple. The gunner merely walks from bush to bush, zigging this way and zagging that, carefully covering every yard of ground from side to side as he advances through the cover. With this dragnet method of combing a cover, no bird will ever get out from behind. What's that? Oh, don't bother about the thanks. It's just part of the service.

What have we here? A grouse flying at a man's head. There must be something gravely wrong with this gunner's technique. Birds aren't supposed to act that way. Well-behaved quarry always give the hunter good shots—straightaway or quartering chances.

This fellow is ducking as though a wildcat were leaping at him. What does he have to be afraid of? A grouse is just a harmless bird weighing only about a pound and a half. It can't possibly hurt him. He should keep his eyes open, so that he can see what is going on. The antics of wild creatures are amusing and often educational. Of course, he can't shoot with the bird that close, because the charge of shot would blow it into little useless pieces. But he should be ready to slam in a barrel when the grouse gets behind him. This, as every gunner knows, is a sucker shot.

Come to think of it, though, the man may not be scared at all; just hiding his head in shame. He probably crowded that grouse into a tight corner where the poor bird had no other alternative than to fly at the guy. Here we are faced by a delicate question of ethics. The true sportsman will always remember that he is pursuing one of nature's defenseless feathered creatures, while he himself carries a lethal weapon. He holds the whip hand, and to take advantage of a poor helpless bird is equivalent to stealing candy from a baby. For shame!

Grousing Is Easy

The next drawing graphically demonstrates one of the commonest gripes of the grouse gunner. On the left we have a bird flying through wild grapevines. That's the way he should look, with all details of feather pattern distinct and clear. You can see the broad tail with its black band, the well-defined pinion feathers, the beady eye and curved beak. We all know that a partridge is constructed that way, and if there is any doubt about it, one has only to study a stuffed specimen.

The drawing on the right is a representation of what some brush plodders claim they see. In the words of one of them: "When a pat boils out in front of me, I think of that dreadful time when I attended the Pithers' cocktail party and lapped up four martinis—on an empty stomach, mind you—when I know darned well that my limit is two. Things began to swim around the room until I couldn't tell the hostess from the maid; except that I have a dim recollection that the maid was a lot prettier. Now, I never drink when I'm out shooting, but I have the same reaction; stuff gets all blurry when I hear the roar of a flushing bird. What's wrong?"

Simple. The guy is excited. He has grouse fever. Never let this happen to you. Cultivate a calm and philosophical mien. Why should you run a blood pressure of 245 just because a silly old bird is flying up in front of you? Ridiculous, isn't it? Reason it out on a logical basis: the grouse is merely a helpless creature, and you are a great big, powerful brute of a man with a gun. You are master of the situation. You aren't going to let that critter make a monkey of you, are you? Of course not! There. Feel better?

Grousing Is Easy

Grousing Is Easy

This one rates high up on the list of tough shots. A much-prodded bird sometimes gets sick of having chilled shot whistle around him and from sheer boredom will take to a tree. Generally it is a thick old pine that offers perfect concealment. At the precisely right moment (right for the grouse, that is) he will thunder out and down toward earth like a jet plane. The noise sounds like sailcloth being ripped.

Gunners complain about the impossibility of this shot. They say that they don't hold low enough, or they stop the gun when the trigger is pulled, or some other flimsy explanation. But the real answer lies in the science of ballistics. A grouse flying at top speed on the level doesn't do much more than forty m.p.h. Give him a slight margin for the added pull of gravity and maybe a little tail wind, and he might up this to fifty m.p.h. What is the velocity of a charge of shot? Better than 1200 feet a second. Ha! Where's your argument?

From this it can readily be seen that gunners who miss grouse going out of trees are merely looking for an alibi. And a pretty lame one it is, for it is easy to prove that the grouse never lived that could outfly a charge of shot. Science triumphs again!

Grousing Is Easy

Oh, oh! This guy is in bad shape. He slipped and fell on his fanny at the wrong moment. Before he can recover, that grouse will be away off in the brush and wild as a hawk on the next flush.

Things like this just shouldn't happen; there's no excuse for such an embarrassing performance. It all boils down to a matter of poise and grace. Consider the primitive redskin; he didn't go bulling around through the woods like a tractor. Obstacles? Phoo! What are they? Such things as jagged rocks, down timber, slippery banks, mud holes, and steep slopes are unimportant if a man is really on his toes. Think nothing of them. Remember the Boy Scout slogan: Be prepared. No matter what your footing, you must be ready to take the shot when a biddie boils out. Never be caught off balance.

If you are naturally clumsy, join a class in aesthetic dancing. Learn to pirouette and leap joyfully into the air. This will be of immense help the next time you have to negotiate a gullied moraine filled with slippery rocks. Or if you think that is carrying it a little too far (and who doesn't), you might practice balancing an olla of water on your head the way the Mexican women do. Practically guaranteed to produce results—of one kind or another.

The problem of making a double on grouse has long been considered almost the toughest in the entire realm of shotgun performance. It need not be. The solution is so simple, so basic, that it is a wonder no one has worked it out before.

Again, science comes to our aid. We have these factors to consider: correct lead, swing, and letting off the loads at the right moment. Let us call them X, A, and B; the result will be Z. Here is how it works:

Two grouse flush from in front of a point. They tear off in opposite directions. The gunner may take the right bird first or vice versa; there are no hard and fast rules. Now if he has studied the factors carefully he is well prepared. He has only to work out the magical and never failing equation—X plus A plus B equal Z.

The result? Wham! Spam! Plunk, plunk. Two shots, two dead grouse. Ridiculously simple, isn't it? What a pity this little gem of mathematical help was not released to the gunning public long ago.

If anything in the foregoing material seems to contradict the title, "Grousing Is Easy," let us clear up the misapprehension at once. It doesn't. Grousing is easy. In fact, it's practically inevitable. Because grousing, according to the dictionary, means something more than the pursuit of a particular game bird. It also means crabbing, griping, kicking, and it sometimes degenerates into plain old-fashioned profanity.

There's no use trying to duck the issue; gunners who know concede that the ruffed grouse is just about the smartest thing in the woods wearing wings. Dumb grouse are all dead—from one cause or another. And the bird's consistently successful conquest is still the toughest problem that the upland gunner has to face.

That is what makes the game so fascinating. No matter how poor your shooting is or how many bad breaks you get, you are ready to go at it again next day. Tomorrow it will be different. You'll make a double, bag your four-bird limit with six shells. Wonderful, isn't it!

Grousing Is Easy

87

Jonathan Woodcock, Esq.

Jonathan Woodcock, Esq.

WHY Jonathan? Well, no reason in particular, except that the woodcock always seems such a sober, dignified old fellow, and Jonathan is certainly a distinguished name. You will find it often in old-time chronicles. It seems to fit august personages, as, for instance, judges. And a woodcock might easily pass as a judge among birds, with his great solemn eyes and dignified bearing.

There is an air of mystery about him, too. His movements are cloaked in secrecy. In some sections he abounds in the spring and autumn flight periods. In other sections, which have almost identical cover conditions, he is virtually a stranger except for an occasional visit.

On a spring day a friend stopped at a grocery store in a small town in the Catskills. On the counter lay a dead woodcock which the storekeeper had picked up under a telegraph line. Several customers were engaged in a lively debate concerning the deceased.

"It's some kind of a woodpecker," said one. "You can see that from its bill."

" 'Taint nothin' of the kind," ventured another. "It's a snipe. I've seen lots of different kinds runnin' along the river banks, mostly gray ones and smaller. Never seen nothin' quite like this one, but it's a sure enough snipe because it's built the same way."

The country around that town has much cover that should afford good woodcock shooting, yet my friend assured me that in a dozen years' shooting in that section he has been able to find only an occasional bird during the season. Not only do woodcock seem to avoid whole sections of the country even where conditions appear ideal, but it is likewise true that they prefer certain spots in a given covert.

In the section of Connecticut where I hunt each fall there are many square miles of what might be termed ideal cover. The hillsides and valleys are wooded with white birch interspersed with cedars. Small brooks flow through many of the valleys, and the ground for the most part is soft enough for successful "mining" operations. Except for occasional stands of beech and maple, small groups of oaks and scattered patch sumac or an occasional abandoned orchard, the country looks much the same. It is typical New England cover.

It would be natural to conclude that one could find birds anywhere in that country during the flight, but, as many woodcock hunters know, such is not the case. I find that certain little patches in a given area of cover will furnish birds, while in the adjoining area, which looks exactly the same, it is a waste of time to hunt.

These spots are usually small, too. I have one such place in mind, not more than 200 yards from the road. It is a little clump of

Jonathan Woodcock, Esq.

birches with a few cedars and scrub oak mixed in. I can depend upon finding from one to four 'cocks there every day during the period of fall migration.

Early in the season there is a pair or more of old birds, "natives" they are called, and usually a brood of youngsters. The latter are full grown, but have shorter bills and are somewhat smaller. These birds are collected by local hunters, and for a few days the spot may be empty. Then, when woodcock begin to move, birds from the North drop in. I found from one to three birds on six consecutive days in this spot. Once I made a double, and on another occasion I was prevented from shooting at the second bird by the presence of an Italian laborer, whom I would surely have collected had I shot. This woodcock took out over an open field and landed in a small patch of bayberry. It was an easy task to flush him again and bring him to bag.

I have found by past experience that, after exhausting the possibilities of this little spot, the next parcel of pay dirt lies an eighth of a mile over the hill. One, two, or, rarely, three birds are to be found there. And so on.

It is strange that birds should consistently pick out small patches of cover when they have so much territory from which to choose. But it is stranger still that young birds, hatched the previous spring in the far-off covers of New Brunswick and Nova Scotia, should be able to find these spots unerringly and ignore the rest. The answer is, I suppose, that what looks to us like good country does not necessarily appear so to woodcock. And the second part of the proposition concerning the ability of young birds to locate good spots undoubtedly is part of the mystery of bird migration.

During the shooting season woodcock seem to prefer hilly sections fairly well wooded, when ground conditions would lead one to suspect that the birds would find slim pickings. It is not at all necessary that water be in the vicinity; some of the heaviest flights are to be found up in the hardwoods, away from the traditional alder swamps often highly recommended as good woodcock cover.

One of the many interesting habits of the woodcock is its practice of going from one cover to another at dusk. Before it was illegal to shoot migratory birds after sunset I waited many a pleasant October evening on the line of flight usually taken by trading birds. It was essential to have a good background, unobstructed by trees or brush and facing the western sky. I could see for only a scant ten minutes or so, and the birds did not move until it was so dark that I could not clearly distinguish detail.

If I were fortunate, I would see Jonathan, or rather his silhouette, against the sky, flapping swiftly and steadily toward me, long bill held at an angle of forty-five degrees. If he saw me move, it was more than likely that he would flare off to one side, out of gunshot. But if he kept his course, I would have my chance. It took nice judgment and skill and no little luck to kill half the birds shot at.

There is no doubt that woodcock are largely nocturnal in habit. Their big, lustrous eyes have good light-gathering capacity, and their love-making and seasonal flights occur during the dark hours and would seem to indicate a fondness for night activity. Have you ever noticed how wild an old woodcock becomes after being shot at and missed? One of my friends swears that they are half asleep during the day.

A great many sportsmen who hunt the woodcock in the fall know little or nothing of his habits during the rest of the year. This little dodger is among the most interesting of our birds from several standpoints, but in nothing is he more absurd and foolish than in his love antics before his mate.

Jonathan Woodcock, Esq.

FLIGHT WOODCOCK, dry point, size 7" x 9", published in 1940, edition of 50

The birds are early nesters and, therefore, come north as soon as the frost has permanently left the ground. In mild seasons woodcock are to be found in late March, and usually the first week in April finds the covers filled. If you will go out on a mild moonlight night in woodcock country and listen carefully, you are almost certain to hear the bleat of a love-sick swain. There is a type of automobile horn that emits a loud, raucous blast sounding like *bee-e-e-ep.* Add to this sound a slight case of laryngitis to make it a bit hoarse, tune it down to about the volume of a spring peeper's note, and you will have a sound closely resembling the bleat of a woodcock.

Now if you possess patience and have good luck, you may be able to learn something very interesting. The bleat is uttered by the male bird on the ground. Somewhere near by is the lady on whom Jonathan is trying to make a whale of an impression. He struts before her precisely as does a grouse, pigeon, or peacock. His plumage is ruffled and his tail spread. With wing tips dragging on the ground, our cavalier wheels and dips and bows as if he were treading the measures of a minuet. Suddenly he springs into the air and with a spiral movement climbs upward to a considerable height, then turns and dives downward.

If you have been able to approach closely without being observed, you will hear a tinkling, silvery twitter made by the air rushing through the primary feathers of the wings. You have undoubtedly noticed that the three outer primaries of each wing are very slender, about one-fifth the diameter of the fourth primary, which is the first normal feather in the wing. Air rushing through these split primaries also creates the whistling sound made by the woodcock's wings when he is flushed in the fall.

These love-making antics are repeated time and again; in

Jonathan Woodcock, Esq.

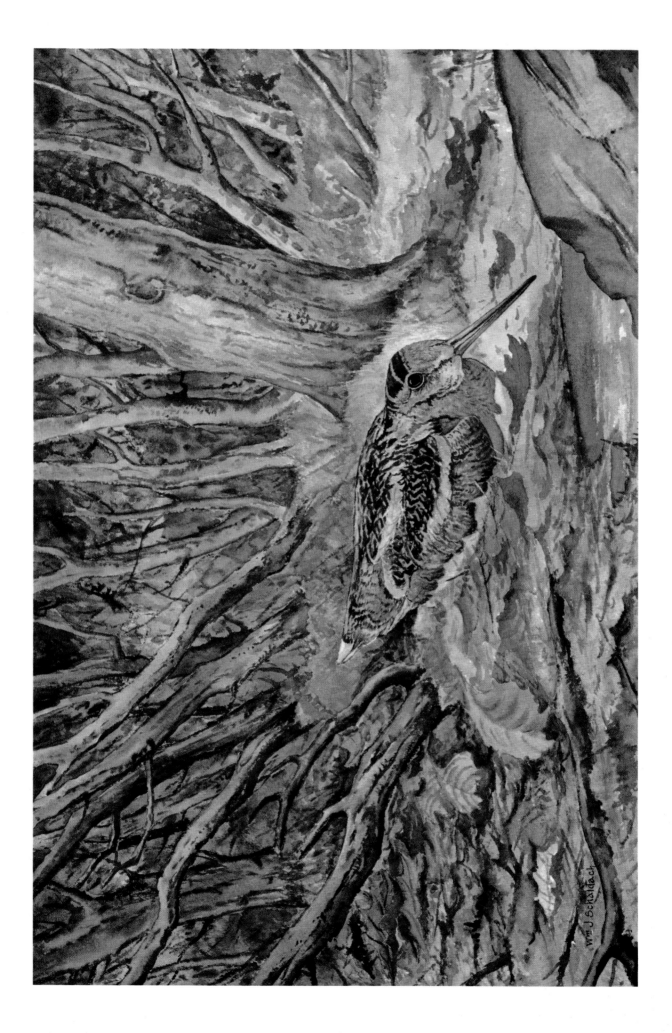

fact, it seems to be an endurance contest. I suppose that the knight with the best technique wins.

When the serious business of mating is over, the problem of nesting and rearing is undertaken. While probably the great majority of woodcock nest in Maine and the southern Canadian provinces, a good number stay in the vicinity of New York and the New England states, Pennsylvania, Ohio, Michigan, and a little west of the Mississippi Valley.

The nest is usually little more than a depression in the earth, made by scraping away brush and leaves. The eggs are four in number, sometimes five, pointed, and very large—a characteristic of the members of the snipe and shore-bird family. They are of buff hue, liberally speckled with coffee-colored markings.

When the woodcock is setting, it is an easy matter to approach closely. Birds have even allowed themselves to be lifted off the nest and replaced, without offering to fly. Nesting woodcock are good subjects for the amateur photographer, and there are many photographs of them in existence. When the young have been hatched, they are unusual and interesting little creatures. Clothed in fluffy down and blotched like a Harlequin, with dark brown bands and spots, they even then resemble papa and mamma, for their bills are well started and their eyes larger than those of other fledglings. The parents take good care of the youngsters, devotedly feeding them well-squashed worms, grubs, and insects.

The question of whether the woodcock carries its young from place to place, either in times of danger or when merely wishing to change feeding grounds, has been the subject of much argument. I have never seen it done, but I understand that it is a well-authenticated procedure, the bird grasping the chick between its feet and legs and holding it firmly until the flight has been accomplished.

Young woodcock begin to fly when quite small, and are soon able to shift for themselves. By fall they are strong fliers and may be distinguished from old-timers only by the smaller bill (usually it is about a half inch shorter) and slightly smaller wings.

In physical structure the woodcock is interesting because of its specialization. The split primary feathers of the wings, already referred to, are unique to the species, not occurring, as far as I know, on any other bird. The aeolian-harp effect finds its principal use in the mating season, when the birds tower in the air and then pitch to the earth. Similar tactics are engaged in by the Wilson's snipe. The wing feathers of this bird, however, are normal, the whistling sound being caused by the two outer tail feathers. These feathers are stiff, and the ribbing, or vane, lies on the extreme outside edge. When the tail is spread to the full extent and the bird dives, the air causes them to vibrate and produce a sound similar to the woodcock's.

The distinctive long bill is another specialization, enabling the woodcock to feed in a manner not possible to most birds. In adults the bill is almost three inches long. The upper mandible is quite flexible toward the tip. In feeding, the woodcock thrusts its bill into the soil and probes around in search of earthworms and the larvae of insects. It can move the upper part of the bill sufficiently to grasp a worm and extract it from the ground. Often the long bill is completely buried. Here again nature has provided for the woodcock in a remarkable manner, for its eyes are placed at the very top of the skull, so that even when its bill is completely buried the bird can easily see what is going on around him and watch out for enemies.

Some years ago I had a remarkable opportunity to observe the feeding habits of woodcock. I was doing some work for a natural-history museum in a mid-Western city. It was about the third week

Jonathan Woodcock, Esq.

in March, and there had been a week or more of balmy, springlike weather. Then a sudden freezing spell came out of the North, bringing snow and shoving us back into January overnight.

About three days afterward a couple of small boys brought me a bird which they had found in their back yard. They said they had tried to feed it bread and milk but that it refused to eat. No wonder! It was a woodcock—so thin that its breastbone stood out like the keel of a yacht. I told the boys that I would endeavor to feed it, and to come back in a few days.

Taking a medium-size wooden box, I tacked a piece of screen over the opening and placed the bird inside. He did not seem alarmed in the least. Then I went out and dug a large handful of worms. I put the worms in the cage and covered them with loose earth to a depth of about two inches. The woodcock observed the process gravely, sitting quietly in one corner. I left him. Returning in about an hour, I found to my delight that the earth was covered with borings and the worms were gone. I dug another handful and put them in the earth. This time I sat down nearby and watched. In a couple of minutes Jonathan got up, shook himself very sedately, and started to explore with his long bill. Finding a worm, he raised his bill high in the air, and with a slithering movement the worm disappeared down his gullet. Apparently he did not make much of an effort to kill the worm first.

I kept this woodcock for two weeks, during which time he consumed an amazing quantity of worms. When released, he was extremely fat and docile. He did not in the least mind being handled and when not feeding would sit motionless for an hour at a time, blinking his great solemn eyes. When the weather warmed up I took him to a piece of alder cover and released him. He flew happily away. I wonder if he remembered his experience.

To Filch a Fish

To Filch a Fish

NO ONE can say with certainty when the caste system originated among anglers, but there is sufficient evidence to show that it is a fairly antique form of folly which seems to grow, rather than diminish, with the passage of time. Anyone who takes up fishing for the first time had better realize at the beginning that he will be popped into a caste, whether he likes it or not.

If he buys a cane pole, cheap line and hooks, and digs himself a can of worms, he's just a fisherman. The elite, high-caste rod wielders will look down their noses at him as though he were untouchable and call him a "plunker" or "dredger." Acquiring a rod and reel will help some, but not much. If he persists in the heresy of using live bait, he's still just a fisherman. To enter the elite angler caste, he must learn to propel and manipulate flies, spinners, spoons, and plugs with reasonable adeptness. Finesse in this art cloaks him with dignity and makes him a respectable member of the craft. He is no longer an untouchable, but he must not think that he has reached the heights. The final estate, the loftiest of all, is that of purist. A purist angles solely with the dry fly. He is not only scientific; he is artful, imitating the ephemeral creatures of the air with consummate skill and making the fish believe that they're the real McCoy. The purist is supposed to represent the ultimate in the art of angling, but for a long time I haven't believed it. The highest caste, in my opinion, transcends all the others. Actually, it absorbs them and goes on to serene heights of its own. I like to call this caste, "the Fish Filchers."

In case this puzzles you—and it easily may—the fish filcher's philosophy is based upon a set of factors involving skill, craftiness, deceit, patience, and cunning. According to Webster, to filch something is to steal it. The idea may be a little far-fetched, but when a skilful operator contrives a method of capturing a fish that can't be caught by conventional means, what else is it but stealing? There is only one question that ever need concern a conscientious fish filcher: Is it legal? Having established that fact, he may—and often does—stray far from the beaten path of standard procedure. Take the case of Caleb Whitcomb.

The people of the tiny Vermont hamlet in which Caleb had lived for nigh onto 70 years considered him the laziest man in seven counties. He possessed a mysterious sixth sense that warned him of the presence of trouble—that is to say, work—and he was invariably absent when there was hay to be pitched or wood to be bucked. At such times it was a safe bet that he was off on some trout stream or in the woods with his old bird dog, according to season. Although

To Filch a Fish

it wasn't considered good taste to side with an obvious loafer like Caleb, the hard-working gunners and anglers secretly envied his way of life—his phenomenal success.

It was on one of his flights from toil that Caleb solved a fascinating problem that had troubled the sporting population of the town for several years. In Granite Creek, there lived a fabulous brown trout. Every one from the butcher boy to the banker knew about this old buster. Tradition had it that he was hatched about the time Dewey captured Manila and was uncatchable because his life was charmed. Several times fishermen had "had holt onto him," but he always tore loose. For over a year the old boy, enriched by the wisdom gained from experience, had refused all lures. Yet he would rise with maddening regularity to the natural flies that floated over his lair.

The very nature of the great trout's hideout made his position impregnable. He had chosen to live in a spot where a ledge of rock overhung a narrow but deep run. The upper end of this run, some ten feet away, was blocked by a sheer face of rock about five feet high over which a small branch of the creek poured. Below the little pool, the water ran through a gut into the main stream where it spread out into shallow pocket water. The high bank above the ledge was thickly clothed with heavy alder brush. The opposite bank, while fairly open close to the water, was within range of the trout's vision. Farther back, more brush prevented a backcast. It could readily be seen that to cast a fly was impossible.

The local fishermen had given up the idea of catching the old walloper; they said it just couldn't be done. Caleb thought it could, and he offered the best possible proof by showing up one evening at the village store with the evidence. It was the old dog in person, with undershot jaw and evil eye. The scales showed a weight of six and a quarter pounds. How was the old campaigner done in?

By a carefully laid scheme, which was, in fact, spiced with a touch of genius.

For several days, there had been a hatch of an insect native to the region. It was a medium-sized ginger with chocolate rings on a plump body, and trout went for it with the eagerness of a kid sucking a lollipop. When the hatch came on, Caleb slipped quietly through the brush and watched the big trout gulp in fly after fly with clocklike regularity. He caught an insect, went home, and tied an imitation that was a ringer for the genuine article.

Back at the old buster's lair, he rigged a tapered leader with the fly, attached it to his line, and laid his rod on the ground at the edge of the alders about 30 feet from the run. In that position and by keeping down low, he would be out of sight of the trout, but he could still see all that went on. He then took the line and walked up boldly to the run, stripping it off the reel as he went. At the head of the little pool a series of flat rocks like stepping stones just cleared the water's surface. The farthest one was in the center of the gentle current so that if a fly were laid upon it and given a quick twitch by the angler hidden in the brush, fly and leader would pop off and effect a perfect drift over the trout.

Of course the fish stopped rising and took to his lair during this trap-setting operation. It would take time for him to overcome his fright and start feeding again, but that didn't matter to Caleb. Time was the commodity he had most of—time and limitless patience. He checked the line carefully all the way back to the rod to see that no twigs or grass obstructed it, stripped a coil or two of slack from the reel, filled a ripe old briar with Mechanic's Delight, and settled back to wait.

Two pipes later, the old walloper started to rise again; cau-

To Filch a Fish

tiously at first, then with reckless abandon, as the succulent insects danced over the run. Caleb listened to the musical "gluck!" of the feeding fish with calm satisfaction. He was in no hurry. There was one chance only, and he didn't want to muff it.

At last the little monitor within Caleb—his priceless sixth sense —told him that the time had come. Stealthily as a lynx, he picked up the rod, raised the tip slightly, grasped the line with his left hand and peered intently at the pool. The trout had just swirled at a natural fly and settled back into position. Caleb gave the rod tip a twitch, and the fly bounced off the rock and started its irregular drift with jauntily cocked wings. It danced and floated along, a foot —two feet—three— It was right over the nose of the old boy when it simply disappeared in a little dimple of water. Then the contest began between man and fish.

Caleb struck gently and jumped to his feet. For an instant line and leader stretched like rubber. Then the little pool boiled with a tidal wave as the fish dove under the ledge. A lesser angler would have lost the battle right there by having his leader sawed off on the rock, but not Caleb. He had it all figured out in advance.

Keeping the rod tip low, he walked cautiously forward and stripped line, right up to the edge of the water. With arched rod pointed downstream, he stepped into the water, thrust a booted foot in under the ledge and kicked the trout. There was immediate and violent action, and a torpedolike form raced through the gut and into the shallow pocket water below. The reel screeched as the startled fish tore off yards of line. But the leader and fly held, and Caleb followed unhurriedly, keeping a steady pressure. After that it was just a matter of playing out the big trout. Away from the security of his accustomed lair under the ledge, he lost his head and soon wore

109

himself down with frantic rushes. Caleb saw that the trout was too big to net, so he simply herded the fish up to a shallow bar and gilled him with strong fingers.

Although Caleb's scheme pretty nearly tops the list of gags used in the fine art of fish-filching, there is another that runs it a close second. I have employed it occasionally and can recommend it highly to the harassed soul who doesn't know what to do about a fine trout that can be plainly seen but isn't buying anything in the way of lures presented in the conventional manner. It sounds incredible, but with the right conditions and plenty of patience you can't miss.

East of Roscoe, above the Forks Pool on the smaller Beaverkill, there are several long and clear backwater pools of cold water. They are fed by springs that come from deep down in the rock ledges and have no connection with the main river except for small outlets. Brush conceals them from the stream, so that a wading angler who is a stranger to the area would never suspect their presence. In August, when the Beaverkill warms up, trout go into the deep pools and the fly-fishing is over. But a few—and there are apt to be some wallopers among them—live in the hidden backwaters.

As may be imagined, these fish are so touchy that they practically verge on nervous breakdown. The appearance of any person would send them milling around madly, and even if an angler remained concealed and cast carefully, the shadow of his line on the water would send them into a frenzy. But they have one habit that leads to their downfall. After the first flurry of panic, they always return to their original positions, usually over sandy bars.

Preliminary preparations took a little thought. I selected a number-12 March Brown wet fly, tied it to a fine tapered leader, and trimmed most of the wings and hackle down fine with a pair of scis-

To Filch a Fish

sors. Then I soaked the fly in mud to make it sink fast when cast. The spot I had chosen was in an opening in the alders near the bank of a large spring hole. It offered a chance for a reasonable backcast and yet afforded concealment. Crawling into position, I spotted a fine brown trout and several smaller ones. The first cast sent them into a flurry, but they settled down by the time the fly had slowly sunk to the bottom. It landed about a foot from the big trout's nose.

He calmed down and finned the water with slow, rhythmical strokes. The battle was won right there; after that it was a game of waiting. A full ten minutes elapsed before I gave the fly the slightest little twitch by flicking the rod tip. The trout wagged his tail violently a time or two, like a dog that has smelled a bone. A few seconds later, another twitch moved the fly an inch nearer the trout. Then another and another. He moved up a little, then backed water and came on again. This was the crucial point, and a bad move could mess up the deal. A pause, then enough motion to make the hackles open and close. The trout crept up close, moving almost imperceptibly. When his nose was about an inch from the fly, I twitched it sharply. He swung and clamped down like a terrier snapping a rat. I struck and there he was, solidly hooked. He was a beautiful fish, 15 inches long, and had I not needed him to give to a friend I would have turned him loose to ponder on the fact that he had been the victim of a swindle. I have taken many trout by this trick when other means failed.

It had been a good many years since I first became actively interested in the taking of fish by screwy methods. The best fish filchers seem to be old codgers. I've met a lot of them, on streams and lakes in many states of the Union and in several Canadian provinces. Once, on a stream in the Lower Peninsula of Michigan, I came upon a whimsical old fellow who toted a cane pole that must have

111

been twenty feet long. He had rigged a reel seat and ring-and-keeper guides to this piece of lumber and had attached a cheap brass reel, loaded with a twisted linen line. That much I could see from a distance. I was moving downstream when I spotted him crouched behind a big pine stump above a pool in the river. Not wishing to intrude I watched as he swung a rig carefully over the water. I assumed that he was fishing with bait. An instant later he gave a heave, and two good-sized brook trout came sailing through the air and landed flopping on the gound.

Walking up, I said, "Hello, nice work."

"Just fair," he replied without much enthusiasm. "Sometimes I git three, mebbe four, at a swipe." Then I looked at his rig and nearly keeled over. Attached to the line was a long leader from which dangled, by means of droppers, at least two dozen flies. They were of all patterns and sizes, some gay, others sombre, spaced a few inches apart.

"What's the idea of all the feathers?" I said.

He stopped munching, shifted a great cud of eatin' tobacco from one cheek to the other, spat, and said, "Well y'see it's this way. I figger if two or three flies on a leader is good, a couple dozen is a lot better. Gives the fish a chance to look 'em over and grab the ones they like best. If you toss this rig on the water jist so, it kinda looks like a big batch of flies had riz up, and trout come scootin' from all directions so's they won't be left out of the feed. Trout is awful jealous, y'know. 'Course you got to handle it jist right. Now you take that little fly pole of your'n, you couldn't do nothin' with it. But with this old bamboo I can really fetch 'em." And from what I saw he sure as blazes could!

That example of multiple duplicity rates high enough to pull in a B-plus, but there is another to which I would award an un-

To Filch a Fish

qualified A. Down in an out-of-the-way corner of the Deep South, there is a lake that is well known for its big crappies. It's a sizeable body of water, and these fish, which are noted for their schooling habit, seem to be possessed with the itch, for they never stay in one place. If you are lucky enough to strike a school you might take two or three fish in rapid succession, then have no further luck for hours, or even the remainder of the day. That is, if you are just an enrolled fisherman in good standing.

But the character I remember so well, the one who gets the "A" grade, was far more than that. He was a squatty little old man, somewhat stooped and hammered down by years of hard toil, but the twinkle in his eyes was that of a boy in his twenties. And his strong arms propelled a diminutive rowboat with ease and grace. When he fished, he seemed to be always on the move, and so far as anyone could learn, he never used an anchor. Old Mose could follow a school of crappies from one end of the lake to the other, up a cove and out of it again, hour after hour, yanking in as many fish as he wished. Since the water was murky and the crappies traveled rather deep, he didn't do it by sight. Those who weren't in on the secret suspected that he smelled them, like a bird dog, or possessed a psychic sense akin to that attributed to the diviner. They were way off the track. Actually the solution was extremely simple.

When Mose started out with his cane pole and bucket of "minnies" he was confronted with only one problem: to catch the first crappie. He would cruise about slowly until he got a bite and landed a fish. Then he had to work fast. Unhooking it carefully, he attached a small black spring clip to its dorsal fin. The clip was tied to one end of four or five yards of heavy black thread; the other end of this thread carried a gaily painted bobber. Chucking the fish overboard, he watched the direction the bobber took and followed by gently sculling his little craft in its wake. The captive invariably stayed with the school, unwittingly acting as a stool pigeon. All the guesswork was removed; wherever the bobber danced, there were bound to be fish, and Mose did a thriving business.

If that seems like a dirty trick, remember that gunners use decoys to lure ducks; and no one criticizes them for it. The path of the sportsman is strewn with numerous thorns—foul weather, bad conditions, and downright hard work—so that any dodge that helps to ease the going a little should be looked upon as a blessing.

What has been written is intended only as the briefest primer to the fine art of snaffling fish by obscure methods that are neglected by standard works on angling. An imaginative person has no difficulty in surmising that the field is vast and worthy of much industrious research. I am thinking of Rex, the kingfisher, and his master.

Rex belonged to an old fellow known simply as Mike. One day when Mike was fishing he found a nest of young kingfishers, and they were such cute, fuzzy little things that he decided to take one home. He hand-fed it on ground fish, and the little rascal thrived.

When Rex was a year old, Mike began taking him along on fishing trips for company. Being a bottle-fed baby, Rex didn't suspect that he could catch fish himself, so he never tried. He spent most of his time perched on a tree branch near Mike, but one day Mike noticed that the bird landed on the limb of a willow overhanging a big pool. Rex craned his neck at the water, chattered loudly, and waved a wing slowly back and forth. Mike had a hunch.

Sneaking up carefully, he spotted a big trout lying at the head of a riffle. He cast a fly above the trout, let it drift over, and hooked the fish. After that it was easy. Rex never bothered with small fish; he scouted out and pointed lunkers. He rarely brought home a fish

To Filch a Fish

weighing less than a pound. But there was one complication. The stream that Mike fished was infested with kingfishers, and he couldn't tell which one was Rex; that is, at first glance. He fixed that by painting a stripe of red enamel on each of Rex's wings. When the bird signaled, the paint flashed like a traffic light and—

What was that? Sounds fishy? Well, I didn't say that I'd actually met this guy Mike and his bird; I said that I was thinking of them. Maybe I never will run across a pair like them, but I wouldn't be a darned bit surprised if I did. At least I'm going to keep on looking.

That's the kind of faith that this mild aberration gives you, once you get into it!

Schaldach

Dark of the Moon

SUNNY RUN, aquatint, size 5" x 6⅞", published in 1937, edition of 50

I F YOU really want hackle that is hackle," Butch was saying, "get it in the fall, after the late-summer molt. Take a young cockerel with bright, stiff feathers and you can tie a dry fly that will bounce when it hits the water. . . ."

He looked around for a response but found none. No one was listening. In fact, half of the fishermen on the hotel porch were fast asleep or close to it. If it hadn't been for Butch's incessant prattle on his favorite theme, fly-tying, I might have dropped off myself —the prattle and the sound of heavy wading brogues clanking along the dusty path to the hotel.

A heavy, oldish figure, clad in patched waders and hung with creel, landing net, and rod, clunked and swooshed onto the porch and sank into the depths of a huge willow chair. The chair

119

creaked, and its occupant uttered a despairing groan which instantly awakened everyone, including Lem Crawford, the village loafer, who was holding down a chair at the extreme end of the veranda.

"Hot, ain't it, Pop?" Lem ventured.

The new arrival just gave him a searing glance and began to peel off his waders. His face was a deep crimson, and sweat oozed from it like juice from a baking Virginia ham. It was not until he had pulled off his waders and filled his pipe that he deigned to answer.

"Hot? Well, I'd say that it's just a little hotter than hell; mebbe two or three p'ints. Just come from Buck Eddy, and there ain't enough water there to make a cup of tea." (Here everyone sat up expectantly, for Pop was a famed teller of tall ones. Buck Eddy is a ten-foot hole, even in the kind of drought we had been having.) "You know what I see there? A couple of trout takin' turns splashing water over each other with their tails to keep their hides from dryin' out. Fact!"

No doubt about it, the weather was unusual for late May. It hadn't rained in weeks, and the streams were dropping fast. Butch and I had driven a couple of hundred miles to the little Catskill town where we were staying in order to have some dry-fly fishing on the famous river nearby. But with temperatures in the eighties and gin-clear water, the best we had been able to do was to take a few small fish early in the morning and again late in the evening. And the maddening part of it was that we could see old lunkers lying in the deep pools—browns and rainbows that wouldn't go in your creel without folding.

Butch and I had almost decided to go home, since there appeared to be no rain in sight. We began discussing it again on the porch, that haven of idle and marooned anglers, when Pop leaned

Dark of the Moon

over confidingly and opined that if we really wanted to catch fish it could be done. It was interesting news, to say the least, since no one had taken anything much bigger than legal size for a month. How, we wanted to know?

"Night fishin'," Pop answered in a low voice. "If I wuz as young as you fellows and really wanted some good fish, I'd get 'em, I bet. But the night air ain't good for my old joints and I don't get around as easy as I uster."

Pop went on talking about the glories of night fishing, and it wasn't long before we had forgotten completely about going home. "The dark of the moon's the time," he said, "and if I ain't mistaken that's what we've got right now." In less than fifteen minutes he had promised to take us out that night and show us his bag of tricks. Creaking joints and rheumatism could go hang.

About ten o'clock we drove up alongside a big pool on the lower river. It was black as pitch as we shut off the headlights and made our way haltingly along the rocky path that led to the river's bank. But you soon become accustomed to the lack of light and are surprised at how much you can see by the dim light of the stars alone. Wits become sharpened, too, and you seem to hear and smell more keenly. And there is just a hint of suspense in the air, a feeling of impending danger against which you must be alert.

As in any other form of angling, night fishing has its own definite technique. Pop was a master at it, and what I learned from him that night still serves as a basis for the several trips I make each year. Butch felt sure he wasn't going to like it—the eternal casting, casting out into the blackness; letting the line and leader drift with the current; blindly picking it up again and false-casting into position to get up to the head of the pool and do it all over again. Butch was a purist, a dry-fly man who frowned on other methods because they lack what he quaintly considers finesse.

Below the rips the pool spread out before us broad and placid, with a gentle current running along the far side, which rose abruptly from the water to a railroad embankment. We had strung up on shore with the aid of a flashlight. Six-foot leaders, tapered to 1X, with a rather large point fly—I chose a No. 6 Alder—and two feet above a No. 10 Gray Palmer. The shore shelved off gently toward the deep water, and by wading cautiously I found that I could reach almost to the embankment with a comfortable cast.

Pop had advised us to wet the flies thoroughly so they would sink, so I rubbed mine with mud. Later I found it a good idea to trim off half the hackle and a third of the wings. This helps greatly to achieve a partly submerged drift. With Pop above and Butch below me I began to cast. The line made a hissing sound as it straightened out over the water, and with practice I got so I could see the faint line of disturbance it made in the indistinct starlight.

"Keep in tech with your line," Pop had said. "Let it drift with the current, but keep the feel of it; don't let it go slack."

Cast, float, retrieve. It was a monotonous business. Cast, float —splash—Zing-g-g! An instinctive strike, far too hard; the wet gurgly sound of a plunging fish. Damn! Just what Pop had told me not to do—tried to yank his head off. A gentle pull will set the hook—like striking a rising salmon. Try to remember that, I cautioned myself, as I reeled in to find a broken tippet with the point fly missing.

Searching for a replacement with the aid of a tiny pocket flashlight—it is better to get along with the minimum of light, and keep that off the water to avoid scaring fish—I became aware of a splashing above me. In the dim light I could make out Pop, rod

Dark of the Moon

arched, reaching for the water with his net. The effect was odd, like a shadow show. There was a quick flash of something white—a fish's belly—a low chuckle, and silence.

Maybe there was something to this night fishing, after all. I found my hands trembling a little as I fumbled around, trying to fashion a Major Turle knot. Fingers must be cold, I told myself, but that didn't make sense, because my forehead felt hot and clammy. Just then a liquid *glunk* out in the pool made me start. That didn't help any, either. I got the damned fly tied on, gave it a good yank to make sure, and stripped line to cast.

The fly dropped into the current and drifted down. I engaged in the business of "keeping in tech," this time with an earnestness born of desire. Cast, float, retrieve; cast, float—confound it, are those cussed trout off their feed? After a while the process became mechanical. The rod came up over my shoulder, line straightened behind me; then that strong, accelerating forward push; the soft squoosh of the line striking the water, the drift, and the pickup.

I fell to musing. How bright are the stars; you don't really see them at all in the city. And that whippoorwill singing his head off over there on the far bank. Wonder what a whippoorwill thinks about, anyhow? Low water, income tax, the world in a mess? Not by a jugful. He just flies around nights, sings his head off, and has a swell time. Not a care in the world. Not a bad life, eh?

We're at the tail of the pool again. Retrieve—cast—drift. Now let's see, where was I? Oh, yes, that whippoorwill. Does he worry whether the old buggy is shooting oil lately? Or how—

Splash—yank!

Good Lord, just about jerked my arm out of the socket! But he was on, and going strong. Down he dashes for the rocks under

123

the embankment. Mustn't let him do that; might saw off the leader. Steady, steady. Now don't get excited. That's the stuff, come to papa, pretty. Easy, boy. Whoa! Now don't do that. Don't do it, I say! Ah, that's better. Play around there where it's safe—for me—and tucker yourself out.

Hours went by (actually about four minutes). Every one of those three jumps was a heartbreaker, but the last was almost unbearable. It's one thing to watch a fish break water in the daylight and quite another to experience it in black night, where you can't see whether your fish is leaping over land or water. Now the net. How in blazes do you net a fish at night, anyhow?

Slow and steady, that's the idea. Don't get excited. Don't— Oh, damn it, will you stop thrashing around? Easy now. Head first, slack the line a little, sco-o-op, up she comes. Boy, what a fish! A brownie, and he must be all of seventeen inches.

"That's a right nice little fish, and you handled him real purty, too," I heard a voice saying alongside me. I started a little. In the excitement Pop had waded right up to me, and I never knew it. His reference to a "little" fish sort of hurt, though. For an average angler (not a purist) like myself, I considered a seventeen-incher something to be rather proud of.

Then I remembered seeing Pop net a trout right after I had lost that first strike. I asked him to produce and he did. It was practically the mate to mine. Besides this, he had another of fifteen inches and a third about a foot long. Nice going, I thought. Where have I been all these years? The virus of night fishing was beginning to bore in.

But Pop didn't seem to be moved. "Good night," he remarked, "but I'd like to see you hit a real big one; like the six-pounder Sims tied into last year."

Dark of the Moon

"Six pounds!" I exclaimed incredulously. "Did he land it?"

"Did he land it!" replied Pop indignantly. "How do you suppose we knew it weighed six pounds if he didn't land it? Six pounds, three ounces to be exact."

That obvious fact hadn't occurred to me.

Then I thought of Butch, Butch the purist, who scorned anything but the floating fly. He would be having a miserable time of it, I feared. Cast, drift, retrieve. The monotony of it would drive him nuts. It had been well over an hour since Butch had departed downstream, to fish the next pool below. It was time for us to look him up.

The sound of our iron-studded brogues clanking on the rocks rang strangely in the still night air. My whippoorwill sent out his challenge again, this time behind us. To hell with poverty, he seemed to say. I thought so, too. It was a swell world, even if the car did shoot oil and there was the matter of the interest on that mortgage. Such things could be fixed—somehow.

We were approaching the pool where Butch was operating when Pop suddenly stopped and pointed. "Ain't that your friend out there in the water?" he inquired. " 'Pears to me like he's tied into something."

And tied into something he certainly was. We hurried as fast as anyone can hurry over rocks and rubble on a dark night and came to the shore where Butch was engaging the foe. His rod was arched and vibrating violently. Hearing us, Butch said, "I'm glad you boys came; I may need help." He seemed awfully calm.

"Flash your light down here in the water and have a look at what I've got hooked. Don't scare him, he's about all in. Been playing him for fifteen minutes."

Fifteen minutes! Shade of Walton, what was it, a tuna?

125

Cautiously I swept the light over the water to a point where the taut line cut in—and nearly fainted. What I saw looked like a canoe paddle. I began to shake.

"Pop," I quavered, "what Butch has got hooked here won't go in a landing net. What'll we do?"

"Why beach him, son, beach him," Pop said softly. "Just a minute and I'll be down."

Down he came, wading cautiously to avoid frightening the trout. But it was hardly necessary, for the big fish was thoroughly licked. It lay on its side, gills opening and closing mechanically, all fight gone. Butch kept a steady pressure on the rod while I played the beam of the flashlight on the water.

We were a considerable distance from shore, but the water was so shallow that it would have been foolhardy to attempt getting the trout in any closer. Pop moved slowly and deliberately. I held my breath as he reached over and slid his great paw of a hand down toward the water. In the combined rays of Pop's light and mine I saw Pop grab the fish by the gills and hold it with a viselike grip. With a sweep of his strong arm he tossed the trout high up among the rocks and rubble.

You would think he would be excited; on the contrary, he was as cool as a bottle of iced soda pop. His comment was: "That's a right nice brown trout, Butch,"—he left out the "little" this time—"and you handled him real purty. I think he'll weigh about as much as Sims' brown—lacking an ounce or two, mebbe."

Butch went over to his creel nearby on a rock and gathered up several other trout. They were just little ones—sixteen- and seventeen-inches. I think he had four, counting the big fellow.

Dark of the Moon

"Whatsay we go home?" he said with a yawn. "I could do with a little shuteye."

Yes, I like night-fishing—the starlight, the song of the whippoorwill, the eerie sound of hurrying water lapping the rocky shore, the glunk of feeding fish.

And I guess that Butch likes it, too. I never could get him to admit it. He says that it lacks finesse, whatever that is. But I notice that he will come along with me on the slightest provocation.

In the dark of the moon there are mysteries, not the smallest of which is Butch.

Wild Dog

THE back-country roads of eastcentral Vermont are perhaps no more intricate or puzzling than those of any other thinly settled gunning country, but there are definite handicaps to getting around. One of these is the Vermonter's traditional aversion to putting up signs that might help to guide the beleaguered wayfarer. If you have strayed and need help, you ask for it at the nearest farmhouse—which easily might be five miles away.

Clay and I were a little luckier on that crisp October morning. He had come up from New York the day before to spend some time in the covers, away from his executive position, which was slowly driving him wild. We had started early from my place in the Pomfret hills to drive to some of my favorite country about 40 miles to the north, a lonely section in the township of Corinth. I had gunned this area for ten years and thought I knew the roads thoroughly, but somewhere in what I assumed was the town of Vershire I got fouled up. Three roads splayed out like a trident, and none of them made sense.

Then we spotted help. He was an old codger with an axe on his shoulder, heading out for a day of savage pleasure in the wood-lot. We hailed him, and before I could speak up Clay hollered, "Where's the road to Corinth?"

That was a mistake. The direct approach is all right in the city, where business is the thing and time is running out; but don't try it on the Vermont Yankee. Clay had said *Cor*inth, with the accent on the first syllable. That was another mistake.

The old boy eyed Clay narrowly, spat a stream of rich brown tobacco juice which sullied the delicate beauty of a clump of asters, and replied: "*Cor*-inth? Can't rightly say I ever hear tell of such a place. Hmmm. Wait a minute. You wouldn't be lookin' fer C'rinth, would you? If y'are, you don't have t'move no further; you're in it. You want somebody in perticler?"

Discretion seemed to be indicated if we were to get anywhere. I was an adopted Vermonter, and though I hadn't lived in the state the requisite 50 years to be completely accepted, I felt that a decade or so might help. So, kicking Clay delicately in the shin to shut him up, I explained about my place in the hills to the south. Then I said we were looking for a character named Hazen. The old fellow softened perceptibly. He came back with a grin:

"Hazen, wal I want t'know! Naow in this country Hazens is as thick as fleas on a 'coon dawg. Matter o' fact, I'm a Hazen myself. *Which* Hazen be you lookin' fer?"

"Clem," I replied, chastened by my obvious oversight in not mentioning the first name.

Wild Dog

"Hee, hee," the man with the axe cackled wickedly. "Reckoned it'd be him. The taown loafer, folks call him. Spends most of his wakin' haours in the brush with his gun and thet bird dog of his'n; or aout on some crick with a trout pole, accordin' t'season. Got a small farm with some caows and chickens, but he neglects it scandalous. Seems t'git along somehaow, though, and never has a worry or care. Naow you take me—"

He rambled on for some minutes, then told us which road to take.

We hadn't been more than a few miles off the track, and after winding through a hilly wooded section the road dropped into a pretty valley coursed by a sparkling stream. The sound of axe blows rang across the frosty bottomland before we reached the house. They were slow, measured, and unenthusiastic. "That'll be Clem," I observed, "putting in time against our arrival, assuming the cloak of industry and not liking it."

Clem let the axe drop in mid-air from an uncompleted stroke when he heard the motor. His expression was that of a man who had been saved from execution at the last moment by a reprieve from the governor.

I had known Clem for several years and had hunted with him occasionally. He was an old-time grouse gunner, woods wise, a fine shot and a thorough sportsman. He loved the game for its own sake, not merely for the meat he got out of shooting. He was quiet-mannered, reserved, and polite—to strangers. You didn't get to know Clem on the first trip; or even in the first season.

The introduction was brief. Clem accepted Clay's proffered hand slowly, appraisingly. They chatted a moment while I opened the trunk of the car, releasing the contents in the form of a big raw-boned pointer named Beans, Clay's pride and joy. Beans wanted

135

out—badly—and didn't fail to show it. In a few action-packed seconds he had chased the cat up onto the veranda roof, sent the family hound packing across country, and missed clipping a big red rooster by only a few inches as it flapped into a bush just in time. Beans responded to his boss's hoarse yell only when he was satisfied that all available livestock had been moved off the premises. Then he lay down pantingly and lost interest in everything.

That's it, I thought, the end of a beautiful day before it even starts. I looked at Clay. He was obviously embarrassed. So was I. It was the first time I had seen Beans in action, and it was enough. Then I looked at Clem. He studied the pointer from nose to tail as he methodically filled a corncob pipe. Puffs of smoke wreathed his face before he spoke.

"Thet dawg any good?" he asked Clay as gently as though he were addressing a five-year-old girl.

Clay took heart and went on to explain Beans' sterling virtues; how he had won a field trial on quail in Carolina; had found and held ten pheasants in one day; and regularly pointed woodcock.

"Now about grouse—" Clay was finishing up.

"Pa'tridge," Clem corrected.

"Pa'tridge," Clay repeated. He was catching on fast. In Vermont there are no grouse—only pa'tridges. He didn't have a chance to finish; Clem was away ahead, and he took up the conversation.

"I don't know nothin' about quail, but I read that you got to hev a fast dog fer 'em. Killed a few pheasants myself, but mostly by accident; we don't hev many hereabaouts, and don't miss 'em. Naow you take timberdoodles—what you call woodcock—they're a mighty poor thing to judge a *real* bird dog by. 'Most any kind of dog—fast or slow—that's got a nose at all will find and point a doodle

Wild Dog

bird. The con-demned things just sit there and blink them big dumb eyes and sometimes almost let you pick 'em up.

"But the pa'tridge is somethin' else again. Hmmm," he mused, "Suppose we try this feller aout."

Clem got his gun and shooting coat and, leaving Bess, his blue Belton setter, in the kennel, we started out. It was to be a day of comedy and immense forbearance on the part of our host, happily crowned by the fickle touch of Lady Luck. The last factor is why this story is being told; wild dogs don't ordinarily make good copy. I'm not mentioning Clay's last name, because he was inordinately sensitive about his gun dogs and the performance of this one might still smart. Clem has long since passed away.

The first piece of cover was a gently sloping side hill, covered with young hardwoods and many alders. Beans milled through the brush in high gear when slipped from his leash and in less than twenty yards skidded to a sudden stop. He was locked up on a bird in a point that was pretty to see. Would it spoil the story to say that this was the only point of the day—by Beans?

Pride of ownership radiated from Clay's face with a benevolent glow. I was slightly dumfounded. Clem's countenance was strictly poker-unreadable. We moved in, and the bird got out on Clem's side. It was a big woodcock, and he took the shot as methodically as though he were splitting a block of rock maple.

"Here," he said, handing the bird to Clay, "put this in your bag; I never eat the things."

It was still early, and the melting frost had made bird scent so strong that Beans simply couldn't help but stop on that bird. He was off again, eating the ground away with long, whippetlike strides. Clay's whistles and calls availed nothing as we followed the creature into a birdy pocket filled with scrub cedar, young hemlock, and birch. The dog had bypassed to one side on open ground—probably because the brush slowed down his rollicking race.

The drumlike roll of flushing wings sounded at a point near the end of the pocket, a hundred yards away. I caught the flick of a wing against the green of a hemlock and followed it. The bird bored straight at me, thirty feet in the air, coming fast. I swung past and pulled as it swept by the limb of a big canoe birch. A shower of white bark drifted slowly to earth—that was all. Then I dimly remembered hearing other guns.

Clem and Clay were coming toward me from opposite sides of the pocket. Each had a grouse.

"They was my flock of young pa'tridges I been watchin' all summer," he said simply. "Lucky thing the dog druv 'em in the right direction."

Clay was devastated by the performance, but was wise enough to see that an apology wouldn't do any good. Perhaps when Beans wore off some steam he would show up better. The problem now was to recover the dog and try to get him under control. Clay and I started off in the direction of the disappearing canine, and Clem headed for an edging a couple of hundred yards away. I suspected that he had marked down a bird and wasn't surprised to hear a couple of shots soon after. He met us on top of a little hill, carrying two more of his brood of young pa'tridges. He scorned Clay's congratulations.

"Like t'kill 'em over a p'int, m'self," he said without any implied sarcasm. "Thet way it's more sporty. And besides, these young birds ain't hardly got no more sense than a timberdoodle. Why, shucks, you take an old pa'tridge like that un I been chasin' fer three

Wild Dog

years, he's got brains; can't afford t'make a mistake. That's why he's alive. Come t'think of it, we'll hev a crack at him next—soon's you kin get in thet dawg o' yourn."

A rustling sound in the goldenrods and joepye attracted our attention. It materialized into a head-hung, droop-tailed pointer, the picture of shame.

"Well, speak of the devil." Clay said, then addressing the abject animal, "Come here, you stubborn, worthless piece of dog meat. I'll—"

"Naow, naow," Clem interrupted, "be easy with him. Tain't rightly the dawg's fault. He jist don't understand that follerin' pa'tridges ain't like raoundin' up quail in a big open country."

The haunt of Clem's fabulous grouse was a mile or so to the north in a region of cutover hardwoods interspersed with small patches of thick hardhack and many edgings of blackberry brush. Small stands of pine and hemlock stood on low rocky ridges, and there were numerous brooks and springs. It was grouse cover at its best.

Beans was slipped again, and we spread out behind him. Whether it was the nature of the tough cover or Clay's constant admonitions that slowed down the dog is not certain, but for a time—a short time only—he performed like an angel. Then hot grouse scent got in his nose, and he plunged through blackberry brush that ripped off his newly sprouted wings—thoroughly and permanently. He busted that bird hard, and it rose with a roar. Clay was just behind, and he rolled it with workmanlike precision.

Pardon me if I confess to a little green-eyed-monster trouble; not jealousy, you understand, but that forlorn feeling one gets when both partners have scored and one's own game pocket is as empty

139

as an abandoned envelope. Maybe my chance would come later, but the way things were going it didn't look like it. It was noon, and fall shooting afternoons are short.

Clay yelled at the dog, but it did no good; he was off again at a wild gallop, and the last we saw of him was a white form, disappearing around a rock ledge a quarter of a mile away. This was not grouse shooting; it was Pandemonium.

We gathered for a conference. Obviously there was no point to going on this way.

"Let's go home and git some lunch," Clem said, still as unruffled as a Yankee town clerk, "an' this afternoon we'll take Bess out an try her. Naow somewhere in thet brush ahead thet big pa'tridge I was tellin' you abaout—"

He never finished it. The dry rasp of beating pinions punctured the still air a few yards ahead. Something that looked like a cross between a capon and a turkey streaked through a maze of birch and hemlock, then broke out into the open, sailed across an old mowing, and disappeared in heavy brush an incredible distance away.

"Wal I swan!" Clem said. "Knowed he'd be hereabaouts. Thet's him all right. Ain't no other sich bird between here and Montpelier."

It was 2:30 before we got back into the cover. Bess, the gentle little setter, rode in the trunk, and Beans had been confined in the kennel at Clem's house. It looked like a peaceful afternoon.

Clem wanted to work out some other pockets before going to the spot where we had seen the big grouse disappear. Bess worked slowly and cautiously through a succession of draws and birdy-looking runs. Soon she found scent, and the way she roaded,

Wild Dog

slowly and deliberately, was good to see. It wasn't flashy work; it was cold and calculating, the kind that proves deadly on that New England enigma, the pa'tridge. Then she locked up in a point. The way her muscles tensed, you knew it was the real thing.

Clem motioned to me to take the shot, and since I hadn't pulled a feather up to then, I moved in. Maybe it was the unique spectacle of a dog really pointing, perhaps just stage fright, but when the bird broke cover I blew off two barrels for a miss. Clem swung on and clipped the grouse just as it was about to flip behind a big hemlock. That made Clem's limit of four grouse, plus a woodcock. Clay had two grouse, and my bag was merely a dose of the jitters.

Bess found game again, this time in a little swampy place. Clem had said that he wouldn't shoot any more; it was up to us. The way Bess was pointing spelled woodcock, and I figured that after my performances, it would be grouse or nothing. Anyhow, Clay was my guest, and I urged him to take the shot. The bird lined out through the brush, a hard shot, and Clay knocked it down within twenty yards. It was a swell job, and I was glad I hadn't shot; I'm sure I would have missed it.

That little blue Belton bitch was a wonder. She went at her task with the smoothness and precision of clockwork; not fast, but certainly not slow. Unlike some dogs we have all seen, she was not a potterer. She wasted no time on obviously barren ground, skimming it over quickly. Her nose told her everything; let the slightest bird scent strike her sensitive nostrils and she was all business. You had the feeling that once she had explored a cover without finding anything, that was it; you might as well move on.

We were working up to the edge where the big grouse had disappeared before lunch. Somewhere ahead he might be skulking,

141

but since three hours had elapsed, he might easily have traded covers and be a mile or more away. Clem looked over the situation carefully and decided to cut well back into the brush, figuring that the bird would probably take to heavier cover.

He put Bess in, and she worked willingly, but could come up with nothing. Once or twice she struck old scent, but soon left it. We went on for a quarter of a mile more and had about reached a point where the cover ran into a point at the edge of a hardhack meadow. Beyond, the country was open for hundreds of yards. This point was heavily wooded with hemlock and pine and very thick ground cover. Seeing a birdy-looking edging, I left the party to skirt along it with the hope of kicking up a stray bird. I was, therefore, in the open when the final curtain fell.

Clem and Clay had been following the dog and were some distance away. Above the crackle of dry leaves caused by my shoes I heard a familiar *Cluck! Cluck!* I stopped. It was the note of encouragement that Clem always used when Bess was on scent. Then it stopped.

Through the brush I could just make out the form of a pointing dog, immobile as a statue, locked tight on game. Could it be the "turkey" himself?

Then—and I blush to tell it—a fascinatingly awful thing happened. I heard a sound as of a whirlwind to one side; twigs snapped

and gravel flew. A white wraith raced past at terrific speed—straight at the men and the pointing dog.

There was a hollow roar as of miniature thunder, then shots and a low muffled oath. The wingbeats approached, and I saw the big grouse streaking at a fast right quarter many yards out. Perhaps it was the memory of pass shooting on duck marshes when I was a lad; or just the instinct that is part of a wingshot, the thing you can't get by reading books. Somehow I knew that the gun had to be away out ahead and kept swinging. When it felt right I pulled. The bird collapsed amid a stream of feathers, hit the earth, and bounced —twelve feet, as I later discovered. I carefully paced the distance from gun to bird and found it to be fifty-two yards.

The venerable fowl was all that Clem had claimed it to be. It weighed two and three-eighths pounds and had a tail spread of fifteen inches, by all odds the biggest grouse I have ever killed.

Being just a dog, Beans never knew, when he dug himself out under the kennel, what a favor he was doing me.

And Clem? Not even this crazy thing could ruffle him.

"Awful purty shot," he said. "Glad you got him. Naow I won't hev t'keep worryin' abaout what cover that fool bird's in."

Then turning to Clay he said, "Come up again to shoot. You won't hev t'bother bringin' a dog. Bess is good enough fer these pa'tridges." If it was a rebuke, it was a very mild one!

ROCKY POOL, dry point, size 5⅞" x 9⅞", published in 1929, edition of 50

W. J. Schaldach

Old Ragged Fin

DRY-FLY WATER, BEAVERKILL, dry point, size 7⅞" x 5⅞", published in 1929, edition of 50

THE members of the Balsam Ridge Rod and Gun Club make no pretense at ostentation. Theirs is a simple code, plainly written into their constitution: "To promote and foster the gentlemanly arts of field sports and angling; to champion the cause of wildlife; to engage in an active program of conservation."

As I was driven to the rugged and sturdy lodge on the club property by my host, an old member of Balsam Ridge, I was impressed by the simplicity of the whole place. There was no attempt at landscaping, such as one sometimes sees. The clubhouse took its place naturally in a grove of canoe birch, near a dashing little river that sluiced noisily through a series of charming rock ledges. At the rear there was a well-kept kennel which housed a group of enthusiastic, tail-wagging pointers and setters. Here, I felt, was the essence of charm and simplicity.

Steeped as I was in this quiet and restful mood, there is little wonder that I was practically bowled over by the sight that met my eyes as my host opened the door and graciously waved me in. It was evening, and save for a few reading lamps, placed near comfortable chairs, the big lodge was dimly lighted. At the far end, however, over the huge stone fireplace my gaze was irresistibly drawn to a blaze of light surrounding what at first glance appeared to be a shrine.

I stopped dead in my tracks and stared. Could it really be? Yes, there in the center of that dazzling illumination, stretched out on an oak panel, was the biggest brown trout I had ever seen. Close to a yard in length, its massive hooked jaw extended a good inch and a half beyond the nose. Even from a distance, the malevolent eye glowered with an evil glint, and the general form and pose of the great fish gave evidence of skilfull taxidermy. But the arresting thing about the monster, the fact that impressed me at once, was the condition of the fins. The dorsal was tattered and worn to shreds, while the great caudal, or "fluke," showed deep rents and tears that extended to the base of the structure.

"Good Lord!" I exclaimed in honest amazement. "Where did that come from?"

"From Balsam Creek, the stream you will fish tomorrow," replied Jack, my host.

"From that little stream!" I gasped in astonishment. "Why, it's unbelievable. It seems impossible. It—"

"I know," said Jack with a grin. "That's what they all say. The stream does seem little, but it has some deep pools, and it flows

Old Ragged Fin

into the big river a little way below here. As you know, there are some perfect busters in that water."

"Tell me the story," I demanded impatiently.

"Why not go up and examine the legend?" replied Jack, who was enjoying my bewilderment with evident relish.

The elaborate bronze plaque under the specimen was even more amazing, in a way, than the monster itself. I quote the unusual information, omitting names, from notes that I took at the time. The facts are as follows:

OLD RAGGED FIN

Brown Trout

(Salmo trutta)

Length, 33½ inches

Weight, 11 pounds 4 ounces

First located May 12, 19____ in the Bend Pool, Balsam Creek, by _____. Two hours' intensive angling with dry fly, wet fly, spinner, and bucktail lures failed to interest the fish.

On June 3 _____ rose the fish to a fanwing Royal Coachman. Leader broke after the first rush.

In the late evening of June 18 the fish was hooked on a streamer fly by _____, who played it for about a minute. Rod joint snapped and fish escaped.

On July 5, after a heavy rain which had roiled the water, _____ set a spinner into the fish's jaw and had the trout on for almost ten minutes. Line became entangled around a rock and fish tore loose, taking leader, lure, and twenty feet of tapered line.

Early in the morning of August 2 the trout was hooked on a deeply sunken Cahill, No. 12, by _____, who reported that a run of six feet to the rock ledge ended the incident on that day.

149

The entry of August 2 ended the chronicle for the year. The monster apparently stayed in Balsam Creek, or returned to it from the big river, for the record went on to relate what amounted to a recital of woes for the next year. I shall not bore the reader with exact facts; one note was as dismal as the next (from the angler's viewpoint). Old Ragged Fin lived on in triumph and became increasingly coveted by the now thoroughly agitated club members.

Two unsuccessful encounters were recorded for the year following, both of them having taken place in early May. The last entry was what the untutored of the land would picturesquely term the "pay-off." Though I have a reputation for gullibility, I rocked back in my tracks and gasped as I read:

Taken on June 5, 19____, by _____. Rod, 4½ ounces. Lure, No. 14 Whirling Blue Dun, dry fly. Landed in 11 minutes.

A No. 14 dry fly! Landed in eleven minutes! I rubbed my eyes and read again, but there it was, as fantastic a bit of information as I had ever seen.

"A number-fourteen dry fly—landed in eleven minutes," I mumbled to my host. "Why, it's impossible—at least unbelievable."

"The fish was taken on a number-fourteen dry fly," he said sharply.

Looking back at the incident, I now see that I was perhaps a bit boorish for insisting on a very obvious skepticism, but the story seemed so fragile, so unexplainable, that I could only say again, "I don't believe it could possibly be done."

The face of my host was as imperturbable as that of the Sphinx. I looked for the suggestion of a grin, the thread of a twinkle, but found none. He was cold sober, like a man under cross-examination, sticking to a well-rehearsed piece of testimony.

In a low and steady voice he repeated, with what seemed

like studied emphasis, "The fish was taken on a number-fourteen dry fly."

It was easy to see that I had gone far enough, but I determined to get the story in full before leaving, if it were possible to do so and remain on friendly terms with Jack. I had known him for many years; we had fished and hunted together in a dozen states, and this was the first time he had harbored any information concerning sport which even hinted of secrecy. It took a real effort of will to refrain from mentioning Old Ragged Fin during the two days that followed, but I swallowed my feverish curiosity and went at the business of fishing with what enthusiasm I could muster.

Balsam Creek has the virtue of being easily waded, a thoroughly pleasant and intimate little stream, with brawling ripples, many slicks where a floater rides nicely, and several deepish pools. These, however, yielded nothing, try as I might with every lure that I possessed. As to the rest of the water, it gave me several brownies a foot or slightly more in length and one handsome fish fifteen and a half inches long. But they ran small, a considerable number not reaching the club size limit of nine inches.

On the morning of the third day, which was to be the last of my visit, Jack suggested that we go downstream to try some water that he particularly liked to fish. I did not know it at the time, but the Bend Pool, former home of the huge trout which was so much in my mind, is located there, about a mile from the clubhouse.

Jack placed me on the stream, with instructions to fish along until I reached a large pool under an overhanging ledge. "You will recognize it when you get there," he said, "by a big stunted hemlock growing out of the ledge. I'll meet you about noon, and we'll have a bite to eat. I brought lunch."

I fished along for perhaps a quarter of a mile with indifferent

151

results. The trout were not rising, and there was no sign of a hatch. The water was charming, but save for slightly more volume and width the stream was essentially the same as above. There was one notable exception. As I rounded a bend, where the stream bed narrowed into a succession of fast rips, I looked out upon what struck me as the most beautiful trout pool I had seen anywhere.

Some twenty feet in width, the clear green water purled along with a pleasant note, to spread into a grand glassy stretch at the tail. Several smooth, "oily" stretches suggested the possibility of big trout, and on the left bank a great jagged rock ledge towered above the stream bed. From the stratified mass a gnarled and twisted hemlock clung perilously to its unusual base. Without being told, I sensed that this was the Bend Pool. What, I wondered, were the exact facts with respect to the demise of Old Ragged Fin?

I was to know sooner than I had dared hope. As I sat on a shelving rock, drinking in the charm of the place and smoking my pipe, a splash attracted my attention. It was Jack, wading through the shallows to keep his appointment. He had a strange wistful look on his face as he sat beside me, like a man who wants to talk but scarcely knows where to begin.

"Your Bend Pool is one of the most charming spots I have ever seen," I said, "and I can readily see how a trout as big as Old Ragged Fin could live here; but how such a monster could be held and landed on a small dry fly is a mystery to me."

Jack was not the least bit surprised that I had recognized the place. And I was right in believing that he wanted to talk. He puffed pensively, stared at a bit of submerged ledge rock near the tail of the pool, and said, "The fish was taken on a number-fourteen dry fly—or was it?"

Old Ragged Fin

"Hang it, fellow," he continued frankly, "I've known what has been in your mind ever since you first saw that mounted fish over the mantle. I wanted to tell you the story right off, but I made a pact with the Judge not to reveal the facts without his consent."

"Who is he?" I asked.

"The Judge," he replied, "is that dignified old gentleman you met last evening at dinner. I introduced him as Mr. _____. Do you recall? He is a justice of the appellate court, but outside of office perhaps the most rabid dry-fly purist I have ever met. To him Halford and Skues are names to be revered along with Blackstone and Webster. He picks up the latest theories, calipers the gut of his leaders, squints at the hackles of his flies in the manner of a collector studying a passage in a Rembrandt etching. It's a religion with him, and like many zealots he has precious little tolerance for those who don't conform.

"Well, it seems that the life ambition of the Judge has been to take a really big fish with the dry fly, something he might talk about and display as incontrovertible evidence of the superiority of his method. Old Ragged Fin afforded the opportunity: the logical processes of a legal mind built up the case. I aided and abetted the thing.

"The Judge, however, has recurring pangs of conscience. Whether or not the trout really was taken with a dry fly, as stated in the legend, is something beyond even his forensic abilities. So, in strict honesty, he has given me permission to reveal the facts, submitting them to the opinion of interested anglers. In that way he hopes to reach a decision concerning the notes you read with such interest. Are they, in other words, the truth, a half truth, or a barefaced lie?"

153

I eased down my waders in the interest of comfort, refilled my pipe, and settled back against a mossy bank of ferns and oxalis. This was going to be good!

"On the morning of June fifth," Jack related, "the Judge and I decided to try the water down this way. It was a gray day, warm but pleasant, and the air had the feeling of rain. I don't think that either of us had a definite intention of trying for the big trout, but it seems that we were irresistibly drawn to his lair. Like a moth to a flame. The monster had been hooked so many times before, had smashed so much tackle, that the members of our club had become all but convinced that the brute was uncatchable. But you know the saw about hope springing eternal.

"On the bank of the stream by that riffle"—Jack indicated the place with a wave of his arm—"and out of sight of the Bend Pool we strung up our tackle. The Judge tied on a number-fourteen Whirling Blue Dun, since he had seen several small flies which resembled it hatching up from the water. He finished first, and by way of straightening out his leader he cast idly across stream to a little eddy, just above the point where the rips spill into the big pool.

"Isn't it strange how a little unimportant incident can create a whale of a stir? As, for example, Mrs. O'Leary's cow, which kicked over the lantern in that Chicago stable. The Judge's cast was closely shadowed by fate. The little dun alighted softly on the slick, floated six inches, and disappeared in a dimple of water.

"Striking gently, the Judge hooked a baby trout, perhaps six inches in length. If he had taken the little fish in at once and released it, there would be no story to tell. But it happened that the Judge had previously stripped off several yards of line, which he had allowed to drop in coils on the bank in front of him.

Old Ragged Fin

"One of these coils had become twisted; so his honor busied himself with straightening out the mess. Meanwhile the baby trout swam into the swift water of the rip and was carried into the head of the big pool.

"The business of untangling the line took some moments, and when the Judge got to the point of reeling in the slack he found that there was practically none left. Attracted by his exclamation, I looked up to see his line well out in the pool and moving steadily toward the rock ledge.

"At first thought it appeared as though the current had carried the line down into the pool, but examination proved that it was actually moving against the current! As we watched we could see the line twitch strangely; then a violent tug made the rod tip vibrate. The Judge struck instinctively. I watched, fascinated, as the split bamboo described an arc, then slowly straightened. This was the calm before the storm.

"The next instant we could see a huge form materialize from under the ledge, turn down current and dash to the shelf of broken ledge rock you see just above the tail of the pool. As the fish passed us its great fluke swirled in the shallow water. It was tattered and deeply rent. The Judge had unwittingly hooked the great trout, Old Ragged Fin.

"For the first five minutes neither of us even dared to dream that this would be anything more than another unfortunate incident to record in the club diary. In the first place, there was that fragile little dun, tied to a mere spider web, a three-X leader. And the rod, while sufficient for a large body of water, would certainly prove inadequate should the fish make a determined dash back to its lair. Why it ever left in the first place is still beyond us.

"The thing that saved us, by giving us a chance to think the

155

situation out, and that proved the downfall of the trout, was the fact that the fish spent its time sulking under a shelving rock. Supreme confidence, I suppose. On one occasion, when the monster did decide to run for deep water, I got in the way and chased it back by splashing my landing net on the water. As the minutes went by we both worried about that leader. Would it hold? Where was the trout hooked?

"It became apparent that something had to be done soon. And it was equally obvious that it would be impossible to land such a huge trout in a small net. The Judge and I talked it over with as much calmness as we could muster, our knees shaking with excitement. One plan after another was discarded. Then, like a great light, a scheme burst upon me. I proposed it to the Judge, who promptly accepted. In times of stress even the resolute have been known to lean upon that bit of fallacious reasoning: the end justifies the means.

"Untying my leader, I made a noose in the end of the tapered line. Because of the stiffness of the enamel dressing, the resulting loop stood out like a wire snare. The huge trout could be plainly seen, or rather the rear half of it, in about six inches of water. Its head was hidden under the shelving ledge you see at the base of that yellow birch.

"Moving very cautiously to avoid alarming the fish, I reached over and eased the loop of line into the water. Fortunately there was practically no current. My task now was to slip the loop over that big caudal fin without touching the fish. If balancing a cup of tea on your knee makes you nervous, you ought to try that sometime. Boy!

"By a supreme effort of will I succeeded in controlling my nerves to the extent where I could slip the loop into place. Once it had encircled the tail, I pulled back sharply. It was like taking a bull terrier out for a stroll on a leash! When the brute felt that line

Old Ragged Fin

on its tail, hell popped. It tore out of the deep recesses of the big ledge in the main pool.

"For a full minute it sulked without giving ground. But, after all, the trout was only flesh and blood; against that relentless backward strain it was soon forced to give in. As we dragged the great trout out on the bank the Judge looked at his watch. Exactly eleven minutes had passed since the fish was hooked.

"During the entire struggle the Judge's little dry fly had held; so he played the fish along with me. We had wondered why it had not pulled out, but now the reason became apparent. It was embedded deeply in the maxillary, the bone that runs along the upper jaw, and outside of the trout's mouth. That explained why the leader was not sawed off by the monster's great teeth. Apparently when the Judge struck, the little fly was ripped out of the baby trout's mouth. At that instant the big fish turned its head slightly, and by the merest chance the tiny number-fourteen hook found a resting place in the cartilage of the maxillary."

Jack paused here to refill his pipe. I could see that he was not yet finished, and I did not wish to interrupt him. But the questions I would have asked were all answered—or rather left unanswered—subsequently by him.

"We were so amazed at the sight of that huge trout," he went on, "that at first we could do nothing but stare and marvel. It was I who broke the ice. 'Judge,' I said, 'accept my hearty congratulations on the capture of Old Ragged Fin. Your name will go down in the history of our club. And you did it on the dry fly.'

"The old gentleman stood like a man in a trance. He just kept staring at that fish, and I had to shake him before he'd reply. I repeated what I said, and I think that only then the full realization of what had happened dawned upon him.

" 'Damn it, man, I didn't catch the trout!' he declared.

" 'But, Judge,' I protested, 'that fly and leader in the fish's mouth—aren't they yours? Didn't I see you play the fish?' Noting the struggle that his honor was having with his conscience, the imp of mischief prompted me. Besides, I wasn't at all sure of my ground in what had all the earmarks of a shady transaction.

" 'There's no use trying to justify the thing, Jack,' continued the Judge. 'You caught that trout.'

" 'I caught the trout?' I exclaimed in a hurt tone. 'Why, no, Judge, I merely landed the trout. You don't think for a minute that I would snare free trout in a stream, even if I were able to, do you? You had the fish hooked on a dry fly and I landed it.'

" 'I like the way you say "had the fish hooked on a dry fly," ' said his honor, assuming a judicial tone. 'You didn't say that I hooked the fish on a dry fly, did you? In court we would term that evasion of the facts. You know that I didn't hook the big trout directly, but through an accident of fate.'

" 'But you were angling with a dry fly, in good faith, were you not?' I parried. 'And as to the method of landing a fish, a gaff is legitimate, isn't it? In some of the muskalonge waters they land big fish by shooting them with a pistol. Why not a loop of line on the end of a fly rod?'

"That seemed to give the Judge an idea. He was pensive for a moment. Then he suddenly said, 'By Jove, in England they use a contraption called a tailer; loop of wire on a flexible shank—same idea as your rig.'

" 'Of course, Judge,' I replied eagerly. I could see that he was weakening; so I followed the hint he had given me, enlarging upon the virtues of the tailer, even though I had never seen one of the danged things, and haven't to this day.

Old Ragged Fin

"After about an hour's talk we built up what seemed like a good case. Old Ragged Fin had been taken, and taken by means of a dry fly. That was it! By means of a dry fly. No one could argue that. It was a good thing to have the brute out of the stream, and so forth. We meant to be perfectly honest about it, but in our hearts we didn't believe in our own arguments.

"Of course, the club members wouldn't swallow the story. You couldn't blame them. In time the whole thing came out. But the funny part of it is that fully half of them contend that the trout was caught on a dry fly. You are the first nonmember to hear the truth. What do you think?"

What, indeed, did I think? After listening to the whole weird tale and weighing the evidence for and against the methods used, I could readily understand the Judge's predicament.

It seems, in the final analysis, that the only answer to fit the case is the one given by Jack himself, on the bank of the Bend Pool: "The trout was taken on a number-fourteen dry fly—or was it?"

TYPOGRAPHICAL NOTE

This book is set in Caledonia, a typeface designed by W. A. Dwiggins and first cut, in 1939, by the Mergenthaler Linotype Company. Dwiggins named his new typeface Caledonia, the Roman name for Scotland, because it was inspired by the early nineteenth century Scotch types cast by the Glasgow type founders Alexander Wilson & Son. However, the calligraphic quality of Caledonia is completely absent in the early Wilson types. For this "liveliness of action" Dwiggins drew on a face cut around 1790 by William Martin for the printer William Bulmer, though Caledonia has more weight than the Martin letters. And unlike the types that were its precursors, Caledonia employs bottom finishing strokes that are cut straight across, without brackets, to make sharp angles with the upright stems. This vertical stress combined with horizontal serifs gives Caledonia its "modern face" appearance.

This book was produced under the supervision of Bookmakers, Brooklyn, N.Y., set by Lino-Flash Typographers, New York, N.Y., and printed and bound by Halliday Lithograph Corporation, West Hanover, Massachusetts.

Typography and design by Joan Stoliar.

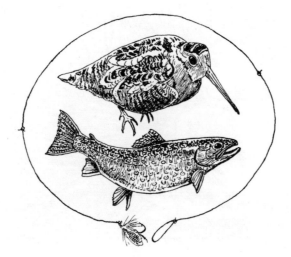